AF521510

Micro, Small and Medium Enterprises (MSMEs) in Emerging India

Micro, Small and Medium Enterprises (MSMEs) in Emerging India

Edited by

Mitali Chinara
Associate Professor,
Department of Analytical and Applied Economics,
Utkal University, Bhubaneswar

and

Himanshu Sekhar Rout
Head, Department of Analytical and Applied Economics,
Utkal University, Bhubaneswar

New Century Publications
New Delhi, India

NEW CENTURY PUBLICATIONS
4800 / 24, Bharat Ram Road,
Ansari Road, Daryaganj,
New Delhi - 110 002 (India)

Tel.: 011-2324 7798, 4358 7398
Fax: 011-4101 7798
E-mail: indiatax@vsnl.com • info@newcenturypublications.com
www.newcenturypublications.com

Editorial office:
LG-7, Aakarshan Bhawan,
4754-57/23, Ansari Road, Daryaganj,
New Delhi – 110 002

Tel.: 011-4356 0919

Copyright © 2017 by the editors

All rights reserved. No part of this book may be reproduced, stored in a retrieval system, or transmitted in any form or by any means, mechanical, photocopying, recording, or otherwise without the prior written permission of the publisher.

First Published: **2017**

ISBN: **978-81-7708-453-5**

Published by New Century Publications and printed at Milan Enterprises, New Delhi.

Designs: Patch Creative Unit, New Delhi.

PRINTED IN INDIA

About the Book

Micro, small and medium enterprises (MSMEs) are the backbone of India's industrial economy. MSMEs not only play a crucial role in providing large employment opportunities, at comparatively lower capital cost than large industries, but also help in industrialization of rural and backward areas, thereby reducing regional imbalances, and assuring more equitable distribution of national income and wealth. MSMEs are complementary to large industries as ancillary units and contribute enormously to the socio-economic development of the country. The sector contributes significantly to manufacturing output, employment and exports of the country.

MSMEs, though important, face a number of problems which have resulted in their retarded growth. Inadequate working capital, lack of information to access domestic and international markets, shortage of trained personnel and obsolete technology are the major barriers to the growth of MSMEs in India.

In the post-WTO agenda, domestic markets have been opened up for imports, creating severe competition for the local industries. At the same time, it has created opportunities for small industries to tap global markets.

The growth of the MSMEs sector must be a central focus of India's manufacturing strategy. This sector is the foundation for a strong manufacturing area providing greater employment with less capital. It has a complementary relationship with large industries because it supplies components and inputs to them. It is the entry point for workers and entrepreneurs who move through it to large-scale enterprises.

The present volume contains 13 scholarly papers, authored by experts in the field, which provide an analytical account of the functioning of MSMEs in India.

About the Editors

Dr. Mitali Chinara is currently an Associate Professor in the Department of Analytical and Applied Economics, Utkal University, Bhubaneswar, where she teaches post-graduate students and guides scholars in their M.Phil. and Ph.D. courses. She finished with highest grades in her Masters class in Analytical and Applied Economics at Utkal University, Odisha. She continued her academic voyage, doing M.Phil. and later Ph.D. in Economics. Before returning to her alma mater as a member of faculty, she taught myriad courses at the undergraduate, graduate and post-graduate levels in state colleges across the length and breadth of Odisha for close to 20 years.

She specializes in economics of social sector, quantitative techniques, econometrics and macroeconomics. With numerous research papers, books and consultancy reports to her credit, she has delivered keynote addresses at several national and international conferences.

Dr. Himanshu Sekhar Rout is the Head of the Department of Analytical and Applied Economics, Utkal University, Bhubaneswar. He has 17 years of teaching and research experience, and has nine books and more than fifty research papers, published in national and international journals, to his credit. He is the editor-in-chief of the biannual journal *Manthan: Journal of Commerce and Management* and a Member of the editorial board of the journal *Utkal Economic Papers*. His teaching domain includes macroeconomics, public economics, health economics, economics of education, Indian economy and research methodology. His main areas of research are social sector economics (health, education, and gender) and intellectual property rights (IPRs).

Contents

Contributors

M.H. Bala Subrahmanya	Department of Management Studies, Indian Institute of Science, Bangalore.
Keshab Das	Gujarat Institute of Development Research, Ahmedabad.
Radha Raghuramapatruni	GITAM School of International Business, GITAM University, Visakhapatnam.
S.K. Mishra	Siksha 'O' Anusandhan University, Bhubaneswar.
P.K. Mishra	Central University of Punjab, Bhatinda.
Andrew Francis	Department of Commerce, St Joseph's College (Autonomous), Tiruchirappalli.
J. Vinoth Kumar	Department of Commerce, St Joseph's College (Autonomous), Tiruchirappalli.
Rushi Pandya	Faculty of Management, Pandit Deendayal Petroleum University, Gandhinagar.
Ashutosh Muduli	Faculty of Management, Pandit Deendayal Petroleum University, Gandhinagar.
Ramakrushna Panigrahi	International Management Institute, Bhubaneswar.
B.P. Mishra	Xavier Institute of Management, Xavier University, Bhubaneswar.
L. Ganesan	Department of Economics, Bharathidasan University, Tiruchirappalli.
R. Senthamizh Veena	Department of Economics, Bharathidasan University, Tiruchirappalli.

Ashutosh Dash Department of Political Science, Utkal University, Bhubaneswar.

Keya (Das) Ghosh, Department of Commerce, School of Finance and Commerce, Amity University, Kolkata.

Setaka Palaka Department of Economics, Berhampur University, Berhampur.

Sandhyarani Das Department of Economics, Berhampur University, Berhampur.

Preface

Self-reliance being the life breath of an economy, micro small and medium enterprises (MSMEs) were accorded the highest priority during the freedom struggle by our statesmen. Thereafter, MSMEs have been recognized as pivotal for employment generation from the earliest days of Indian Independence. Besides having a low capital and technology requirement, MSMEs use traditional or inherited skills and local resources, and the export potential of products they produce is quite high.

In India, MSMEs account for more than 80 percent of total industrial enterprises, produce over 8,000 value-added products and employ an estimated 60 million people. They contribute around 45 percent to the manufacturing output and about 40 percent to exports. In addition, over 50 percent of MSMEs are rural enterprises and widely distributed across low-income states making them an important sector for promoting economic growth and poverty reduction. The sector is instrumental in bringing about a more equitable distribution of income and wealth, thereby making the growth process more broad-based and inclusive.

Against this backcloth, this book brings together scholarly perspectives on MSMEs in India and their prospects and challenges. This will be a recommended text for all those interested in understanding the contemporary trends around MSMEs in India and prognosis of their future.

In this connection, we are deeply indebted to numerous individuals and several institutions for their kind help in putting this book together—for, without their advice and assistance, this compilation would have never seen the light of the day.

The greatest quantum of debt is owed to the authors of individual chapters, who have been patient and co-operative in imparting a distinctive scholarly quality to this publication.

Our patron, Professor Asoka Kumar Das, Hon'ble Vice Chancellor, Utkal University has been a source of unceasing inspiration and unparalleled encouragement in all our academic initiatives. Our Advisor, Professor Ranjan Kumar Bal, Chairman P.G. Council has tendered valuable advice on vital matters, which significantly improved the conceptual integrity of this publication.

Our colleagues, Siba Sankar Mohanty, Aparajita Biswal, Alok Ranjan Behera, Swayam Prava Mishra and Atal Bihari Das have been unstinting in their help in co-ordinating myriad aspects of this publication, and have truly been force multipliers in our efforts. The students and administrative staff of our Department of Analytical and Applied Economics have been tireless and diligent in their support.

We have received an enormous deal of energy and benefaction from Khadi and Village Industries Corporation, Coir Board of India, National Bank for Agriculture and Rural Development (NABARD), Tata Steel and Mahanadi Coal Fields. We sincerely thank them for their gracious patronage and admire them for their commitment to furthering academic exploration.

Finally, we express our thanks to the entire editorial team of New Century Publications, New Delhi especially Mr. Sandeep Sury, for their meticulousness and cooperation in bringing this book to its current avatar.

Mitali Chinara
Himanshu Sekhar Rout

1

MSMEs: Introduction and Overview

Mitali Chinara and Himanshu Sekhar Rout

Introduction

The revolutionary poet Aurobindo Ghose famously stated in the early 1900s that 'political freedom is the life breath of a nation'. It would not be an overstatement, then, to say that self-reliance is the life breath of an economy. In recognition of this, our statesmen accorded micro, small and medium enterprises (MSMEs), or the village and small industries (VSIs), as they were referred to then, the highest priority during the freedom struggle. Khadi not only became a political symbol, but more importantly an emblem of economic self-reliance and a tool for rebuilding the Indian economy. Thereafter, MSMEs have been recognized as pivotal for employment generation from the earliest days of Indian Independence. Besides, MSMEs have low capital and technology requirements; they use traditional or inherited skills and local resources, and the export potential of products they produce is quite high. That they play a pivotal role in the economic and social development of the country was acknowledged well before the planning era, when the National Planning Committee documents were prepared in 1938.

In India, MSMEs have been defined on the basis of historical value of an enterprise's investment in plant and machinery, which is one of its kind in the world in the sense that in other countries of the world, employment size and/or annual turnover are used as variables to classify enterprises. Going by this criterion of investment ceiling, the limits for micro and small units have regularly gone up over the years, and more so during the post-reforms period. The idea to promote export orientation by the MSMEs is also clearly etched in policy when the category was explicitly introduced in 1991. However, the most significant aspect of definitional changes has been the inclusion of 'medium' enterprises through the Micro, Small and Medium Enterprises Development (MSMED) Act of 2006. As per this Act, the investment limit (in plant and machinery) for micro small and medium enterprises in the manufacturing sector is ₹ 20 lakh, ₹ 5 crore and ₹ 10 crore respectively, and in service enterprises it is ₹ 10 lakh, ₹ 2 crore and ₹ 5 crore respectively.

The Plan-based strategy of industrialization that our nascent nation adopted was based on two principal pillars, of which reservation of employment intensive industries in the small-scale sector was one. Policy measures included fiscal concessions, subsidized and directed bank credit, and technical and marketing support, along with reservations of products for exclusive production by the SSI sector. The policy of reserving products for exclusive manufacture in the small-scale sector was started in 1967 with 47 items; the list of reserved items rose to 873 in 1984. Since the mid-1980s there was a gradual turnaround in policy, including reforms in the tax system and liberalization of import policy. The number of items on the reserved list for the SSI sector was brought down to 836 by 1989, 605 by 2005 and finally the reserved list was done away with in April 2015.

The changing winds and shifting sands with the onset of reforms of 1991 necessitated an alternative approach to engendering the growth of MSMEs. Consequently, the focus of fiscal efforts shifted from a protectionist regime to a promotional campaign, enabling MSMEs to upgrade their technology, upskill their labour, improve their product offerings and seek out new markets. As per the Economic Survey 2014-15, 3.61 crore MSMEs contribute 37.5 percent of the country's GDP, employ 805.24 lakh people and contribute to the tune of 44.70 percent of India's exports.

In addition, over 50 percent of MSMEs are rural enterprises and widely distributed across low-income states making them an important sector for promoting economic growth and poverty reduction. The sector is instrumental in bringing about a more equitable distribution of income and wealth, thereby making the growth process more broad-based and more inclusive. The extent of inclusivity of the sector can be assessed from the fact that nearly 50 percent of the units are owned and operated by the disadvantaged sections of the society. In recent years, the MSME sector has consistently registered higher growth rates as compared to the entire industrial sector. The sector has also exhibited praiseworthy adaptability to sustain itself during periods of economic downturn and recession.

It is well recognized in policy circles that MSMEs have a critical role in boosting industrial growth and generating avenues for gainful and productive employment, in an economy marked by sluggish employment growth. Additionally, MSMEs play a crucial role in achieving empowerment of the rural workforce, boosting the overall prospects of weaker sections and attaining equitable distribution of incomes.

Acknowledging the pervasive significance of MSMEs in the Indian economy, the government has initiated a plethora of schemes for establishing new MSMEs and bolstering of existing ones. These include:

- Prime Minister's Employment Generation Programme.
- Micro and Small Enterprises Cluster Development Programme.
- Credit Guarantee Fund Scheme for Micro and Small Enterprises.
- Performance and Credit Rating Scheme.
- Assistance to Training Institutions.
- Scheme of Fund for Regeneration of Traditional Industries.

A Task Force was constituted by the Prime Minister in 2009 to delve into issues which inhibit the growth of the sector. The Task Force made 85 recommendations. Subsequently, the Planning Commission constituted a Working Group on MSMEs Growth for Twelfth Five Year Plan (2012-17) in May 2011. The Group was asked to suggest specific action plans and milestones to be achieved during the Twelfth Plan besides carrying forward the recommendations of the Prime Minister's Task Force. More recent initiatives such as Stand Up India Scheme, MUDRA Yojana and enhancement of the corpus and coverage of Credit Guarantee Trust Fund for Micro and Small Enterprises are expected to impart further momentum to the MSME juggernaut.

Globalization, which marks a shift from earlier policy of controlled industrialization—with protection to domestic industries along with import substitution measures—has provided the sector a wider market and access to better technology, while exposing it to ruthless competition from larger players, both domestic and multinational. To ensure a firm ground to the sector in the global market place, Government of India has put a number of initiatives in place. Going by the official statistics, the MSME sector has performed well in the post-reforms period in terms of the number of enterprises, employment and value of output, though the average size of the enterprises (employment per enterprise) has remained at 2.4, throughout the period from 1990 to 2006. This points a finger towards the very small size of the units which will have implications for their production capability and efficiency. The export performance of the sector has also been quite impressive.

In spite of the several initiatives undertaken by the government from time-to-time, the MSME sector has been burdened with several maladies which have not only stunted the growth of existing units, but also prohibited new entrepreneurs from venturing into the sector.

Overview of the Volume

M.H. Bala Subrahmanya in his paper, *Development of SMEs in India: Policies, Performance and Prospects* attempts to throw light on the origin and evolution of India's SME policy since evolution and to examine its growth performance since 1990-91. The paper also explores the growth prospects of the sector in the future to bring out policy imperatives. Given the three phases of policy evolution, namely protection and promotion till 1990-91, promotion of competitiveness and dilution of protection from 1990-91 to 2005-06 and irrelevance of protection and enhancement of competitiveness thereafter, the performance of the sector seems to have improved relatively since 2005-06, in spite of exhibiting some degree of unsteadiness. However, the increasing reliance of SMEs on the international market and fluctuations in the global export performance largely explained the unsteady growth performance.

He recommends the 3-Is strategy to ensure a steady growth of SME sector, i.e. promotion of Inter-firm/institutional linkages, Innovation and Internationalization for achieving better quality and productivity to penetrate the international market steadily.

Keshab Das in his paper, *MSMEs in India: Challenges of Informality and Globalization* points out that industrialization in India has been marked by the preponderance of micro, small and medium enterprises, particularly in terms of their contribution to job generation and addressing regional disparities in growth. The growth of the MSME sector in India has invalidated the Andersonian prognosis that small enterprises would, eventually, give way to the scalar advantage of the large. In globalizing India, MSMEs have come to capture the imagination of policy makers, development practitioners and global players. An impressive repertoire of small firm development policy notwithstanding, the sector's performance during the economic reforms period, which has overemphasized external orientation, has been particularly worrisome. The overwhelming presence of informality in both the production and labour processes has serious implications for sustainability and competitiveness. On the other hand, with the deepening of the engagement of Indian MSMEs with global buyers, often forming part of a preferred conduit of bilateral trade and investment agreements, global production networks have emerged as new challenges in the organization of production. The paper deals with these issues from a policy perspective.

Radha Raghuramapatruni in her paper, *Opportunities and Challenges for the Growth of MSMEs in India* opines that the Indian MSME sector plays an integral part in the growth of the economy by showcasing Indian entrepreneurship to the world and hence is the engine of economic growth for India. There are about

30 million SMEs in India which employ more than 60 million people by creating massive amount of jobs year upon year. After agriculture, small business is the second largest employer of human resources in the country. However, the SMEs are facing myriad challenges in the current scenario which, if not addressed, pose risk to the high growth trajectory. The paper is an attempt to focus on the present status and performance of MSMEs in India and the future prospects.

S.K. Mishra and P.K. Mishra in their paper, *Dynamic Nexus between MSME Sector and Economic Growth in India* hypothesize that the growth of MSMEs can positively contribute to the real economic growth of the Indian economy. They have evaluated the performance of MSME sector, and also examined the dynamic nexus between the growth of MSME sector and the real economic growth of India using Dynamic OLS regression in the presence of non-stationary time series variables. The results provide the evidence of positive impact of MSME sector on long-run economic growth of India.

The MSME sector in India is highly heterogeneous in terms of the size of the enterprise, variety of products and services offered and the levels of technology employed. While one end of the MSME spectrum contains highly innovative and high growth enterprises, the other end has more than 94 percent of MSMEs unregistered, with a large number established in the informal or unorganized sector. As per the estimates and statistics, out of 26 million MSMEs, only 1.5 million are registered and the remaining remain unregistered.

Andrew Francis and J. Vinoth Kumar in their paper, *Micro, Small and Medium Enterprises: Priceless Diamonds Craving for Polishing* argue that marketing is a strategic tool for business development, and is the most important factor for the success of any enterprise, and it is all the more critical in the case of the growth and survival of micro, small and medium enterprises.

Rushi Pandya and Ashutosh Muduli in their paper, *Internationalization and Innovation in Indian SMEs: A Study of Indian IT Sector* point out that one of the pillars of the growth of the Indian economy has been the information technology (IT) industry, which contributes 8.1 percent to the country's GDP. The IT industry in India has grown at an average rate of 13.1 percent between 2008 and 2014. According to a NASSCOM Report, there are more than 3,100 IT-based new ventures in India, being the third largest entrepreneurial ecosystem in the world. With an annual growth rate of 26 percent, around 11,600 new IT-based ventures are expected in India by the year 2020. Many SMEs from India have expanded their services and products to different countries.

Most of the SMEs are integrating internationally by developing import-export units in one or more countries. With the pressure of competition, SMEs are required to perform consistently. Expectations of higher quality by the customers and tighter cost control strategies by SMEs make innovative processes important. Innovation for SMEs is very important as it gives them an edge over the market. Their paper explores the challenges faced by IT-based new ventures during the phase of scale-up or expansion for internationalization. Further, an attempt has been made to capture the issues and challenges for adopting innovation by such firms.

Ramakrushna Panigrahi in his paper, *Financing of Micro Enterprises: Challenges and Prospects* argues that the sector often faces lack of quality credit facility due to small size of business, despite the rhetoric and various government schemes to address the issue of availability of formal credit at low cost that is suitable to the credit appetite of the entrepreneurs. His paper is an attempt to analyse the issues in financing the MSMEs and its profitability from a competitive market environment perspective.

B.P. Mishra in his paper, *Burden of Risk-based Pricing by Financing Banks on SMEs* uses two regression models, one relying solely on quantitative information (from the analysis of financial ratios) and the other additionally including qualitative information (credit analyst's judgments on management quality, business risk, account behaviour, regulatory compliance etc.), the results of which have been compared. The study, using statistical tests, determines whether the distributions differ significantly, applied on an extensive set of "real world" assigned credit rating data of a particular bank. The data also have been tested through ANOVA (Divergence) analysis. The value of divergence (both mean and standard deviation) is significant, implying that the bank has assigned higher rating than justified by the units diluting the risk estimation and consequently the risk capture.

The study contributes to the SME rating literature in the Indian context and it explains that subjective judgments are indeed capable of yielding valuable information and improve credit rating systems which are based solely on quantitative information by considerable degree. Secondly, default risk is most likely not homogenous within internal rating classes. Banks, according to him, have not implemented internal borrower risk-rating systems in such a way that they result in consistent estimates of portfolio credit losses. Risk (defined in terms of portfolio shares of internal rating grades) is widely varied and if, loan pricing is linked to credit risk, SMEs will be further worse off in getting bank finance.

L. Ganesan and R. Senthamizh Veena in their paper, *Progress and Prospects of MSMEs in Tamil Nadu* focus on the MSMEs in the state of Tamil Nadu. The MSME sector has a major contribution to the economy of Tamil Nadu. The State Industrial Profile, 2014-15 of Tamil Nadu reveals that, Tamil Nadu accounts for 14.95 percent of the total number of operational MSMEs in India. Also, 15.24 percent of India's micro enterprises are located in the state which is the highest among all states. While analyzing the progress of the MSMEs in Tamil Nadu, the paper also attempts to study the problems and prospects of MSMEs in the state. On the whole, the researchers have highlighted the potential of MSMEs in generating employment, reducing poverty, increasing production in the state and call for close attention from the Central and State Governments to regulate and encourage MSMEs.

Ashutosh Dash in his paper, *Women Entrepreneurs in Micro, Small and Medium Enterprises in Odisha* has presented the results of a case study of women engaged in *badi*-making in Keonjhar District of Odisha. The study reveals that there is widespread illiteracy among the women engaged in this activity and there is a need to up-skill them and provide them with marketing support which will enhance their productivity and efficiency. They also need training in rudiments of book keeping and accounting so that they can better manage their finances.

Keya (Das) Ghosh in his paper, *Rural Handicraft Artisans* points out that Indian rural market has revealed some remarkable trends and developments. Four consecutive years of positive growth in rural GDP has not just boosted sentiments but also the spending power there. However, on the flip side, the rural producers/artisans have not benefited much from the entire process of growth. His research is confined to rural micro entrepreneurs and small business communities of West Bengal who deal with handicrafts and handlooms. The author attempts to understand and analyze the marketing problems and issues of rural micro entrepreneurs and producers from various parts of the Indian sub-continent in general and West Bengal in particular.

Setaka Palaka and Sandhyarani Das in their paper, *Growth and Performance of MSMEs* have made a study of the nature and trend of growth of MSMEs since the introduction of economic liberalization in Odisha. The analysis takes into account the registered units, their investment and employment, both for the current years and the cumulative figures for all the 30 districts of the state. It has been found that the districts which have many large-scale industries, like Sundargarh, Jharsuguda and Jajpur, have a good number of MSMEs too. The coastal districts, like Ganjam, Khorda and Cuttack, also have large number of small enterprises. Interior districts, like Boudh, Gajapati, Kondhamal, Malkangiri, Nabangpur, Sonepur and Sambalpur, are not so favourably placed in terms of the number of MSMEs. However, all the districts and the state as a whole have registered significant positive growth in respect of the chosen indicators of MSMEs, such as registered units, investment and employment.

We take this opportunity to place on record our deep

appreciation and gratefulness to all the contributors to this volume. Their scholarly contributions would surely add to the existing body of literature on MSMEs in India.

2

Development of SMEs in India: Policies, Performance and Prospects

M.H. Bala Subrahmanya

Introduction

Firm size spectrum varies from micro firms on the one end, to small firms, medium firms, large firms and MNCs/TNCs on the other. Most firms emerge as start-ups and depending on their survival, success and growth rate, their size is determined. However, start-ups may emerge in any form from micro size to a large size, though majority of them emerge as micro start-ups. Given their time of inception, form of birth and rate of growth, firms of varying sizes thrive in the industrial sector of an economy.

In general, firms have a high mortality rate in the initial years of their birth and subsequent operations, as they encounter various constraints for their day-to-day operations. According to the SBA Office of Advocacy (2014, p. 1), "About half of all new establishments survive five years or more and about one-third survive 10 years or more. As one would expect, the probability of survival increases with the firm's age. Survival rates have changed little over time".

However, firm failure and exit from the market has several economic and social consequences: unemployment, loss of production, investments etc. It is to avoid these undesirable consequences, among others, that start-ups and micro firms are in general provided support of various kinds. This holds good for industrialized as well as industrializing economies. More often, policy support is extended beyond the micro phase of a firm's life. Broadly, exclusive policy support is extended to micro, small and medium enterprises. These smaller size firms are often clubbed together, and are called "small and medium enterprises or SMEs". To extend policy support to SMEs, it is essential to define them exclusively and differentiate them from the rest of the industry.

SMEs: Definition, Significance and Benefits

In general, SMEs can be defined in terms of firm size or firm ownership. Firm size can be defined in terms of factor inputs such as land, labour, and capital investments or in terms of output such as annual sales turnover or in terms of annual balance sheet. Firm ownership refers to number of owner founders and nature of the organization. Given this, SMEs are defined in different ways in different countries and at different times. Although there is a significant variance in the countries' definitions of SMEs, around a third of the countries define SMEs as having up to 250 employees (Kushnir, et al., 2010). The core objective of defining SMEs is to segregate them from the rest of the industry for extending policy support for exclusive promotion.

SMEs have a visible presence in most economies, in terms of their contribution to key macroeconomic variables such as national employment, GDP, and national exports, among others. They make up for more than 90 percent of businesses worldwide and account for almost 60 percent of employment (UNIDO, 2002). SMEs are a fundamental part of the economic fabric in developing countries, and they play a crucial role in furthering growth, innovation and prosperity. SMEs include a wide range of businesses, which differ in their dynamism, technical advancement and risk attitude. Many are relatively stable in their technology, market and scale, while others are more technically advanced, filling crucial product or service niche. Others can be dynamic but high-risk, high-tech "start-ups". Researchers and practitioners agree that SMEs are crucial contributors to job creation and economic growth in both high and low-income countries (Dalberg, 2011).

If SMEs deserve an exclusive segregation for policy promotion, it is because they bestow on an economy multiple benefits. They generate employment from technically qualified to skilled to unskilled labourers. They require a lower investment per unit of enterprise, rely less on infrastructure and therefore can be easily dispersed into wider locations to achieve balanced regional industrial development. They are the means of entrepreneurship nurturing and can be the means as well as outcomes of innovation. Given these qualities, they lend greater stability to industry and the economy.

Why Do SMEs Emerge, Sustain and Grow?

Theoretically, three important factors can be attributed to the spring-up, survival and growth of SMEs (Anderson, 1982):

- Locational influences.
- Process influences.
- Market influences.

When the level of income is low, infrastructure is underdeveloped, markets are small and dispersed, small-scale production to make use of local resources and local skills to meet local needs is an efficient option. It is these *locational influences* which cause the generation of multiple small-scale firms in rural, semi-urban and even urban areas. However, when the level of income starts rising, with infrastructure development when markets expand and grow, locational influences start declining, leading to either a gradual growth of small-scale firms or emergence of larger firms combined with a steady decline of small-scale firms. A steady decline of locational influences gives scope for the emergence of a competitive relationship between small and large firms. Locational influences are likely to be stronger in the initial stages of economic development but tend to decline as and when a country progresses on the path of economic development.

Some production activities can be efficiently undertaken if the production processes are segmented and different production tasks are undertaken by firms of different sizes. Such production activities give scope for complementary relationship between large and small firms. Automobiles, electronics and machine-building activities come under this category where parts and components are manufactured by SMEs whereas assembling of final products is done by large firms. These are called *process influences*, which are primarily responsible for the emergence and sustenance of sub-contracting or ancillary relationship of SMEs with large firms. Process influences are likely to be negligible in the initial stages of economic development but inter-firm relationship (in the form of sub-contracting) is likely to get strengthened with the progress of economic development.

For certain products, total markets are small, irrespective of the level of income, size of population, level of infrastructure development, etc. These include handicrafts, specialized jewellery, high-end consumer products, etc. As a result, to cater to the demand for such products, small-scale production is the best option. These are *market influences*, which give scope for the independent existence of SMEs in every economy, irrespective of the stage of economic development. Therefore, even with the progress of economic development, market influences are likely to sustain.

With the advent of ICT revolution, technology is assuming growing prominence in the generation of technology-based start-ups, which led to the fourth factor, namely, technological influences. When technology emerges but changes rapidly, small-scale operation to begin with, becomes a viable option. But when technology gets stabilized or gets acceptance from the market on an increasing scale, such small-scale firms grow at differential rates, to become medium or large-sized firms. These are *technological influences* which nurture and promote technology based start-ups. They tend to cease to be small-scale firms within a short period of time, due to their accelerated rate of growth or due to their exit (due to unviability) (Bailetti, 2012).

Finally, SMEs are means of expression of entrepreneurship—for prospective entrepreneurs with different income levels. In general, people from poor income households (low income groups) who have little education and skills, take advantage of locational influences and initiate livelihood based entrepreneurship for household industries, rural artisans, and unregistered workshops (traditional industries/services). People from middle income groups with higher levels of education and skills, make use of either locational influences or process influences or market influences, utilize government policy support and begin policy induced entrepreneurship for modern small-scale industries/services. People from middle income/high income groups with techno-managerial qualifications and wider exposure to national and international contexts, make use of ICTs leading to technology/innovation led entrepreneurship to exploit technological influences for technology based start-ups (Bala Subrahmanya, 2015).

Exclusive Policy Support for SMEs: Rationale

If there are some factors, natural or otherwise, which encourage and support SMEs, where is the need for an exclusive policy support for SMEs? Policy support would call for government machinery on the one hand and devotion of scarce resources of an economy, on the other. Will it be a superfluous exercise? Certainly not.

Of course, SMEs would spring-up periodically in different locations due to various factors discussed previously but they face innumerable constraints for their day-to-day operations and growth. Firstly, market forces are not conducive for SME operations and growth relative to large firms. This is true with respect to the availability of finance, markets, human resources, technology, etc.

Secondly, SMEs are too significant quantitatively to be ignored in any economy. Thirdly, encouraging their birth, functioning and growth brings innumerable benefits to economy and society. Finally, their healthy growth can be a vital instrument for industrial transformation and economic development in the medium to long-run.

SMEs in India

SMEs (earlier known as village and small scale industries) had a special appeal for all those who had a concern for India's future development much before Independence. That is why they found an immediate response from the policymakers soon after Independence. The Industrial Policy Resolution (IPR), 1948 followed by the Industrial Policy Resolution (IPR), 1956 attached a special role to the sector as it was particularly suited for better utilization of local resources and for achievement of self-sufficiency with respect to certain consumer goods (Kulkarni, 1991). Those days, SMEs comprised of two sub-sectors: (i) traditional industries and (ii) modern small-scale industries. The former included primarily, khadi and village industries, handlooms, handicrafts, whereas the latter consisted of small-scale industries and power looms.

If SME sector has grown from strength to strength since Independence, it could be attributed to: (i) natural factors, (ii) policy initiatives and (iii) response from market forces. While natural factors have been briefly touched upon earlier, and market forces are largely reactive to policy initiatives, it is pertinent to understand the extent and intensity of policy support extended to the sector since Independence.

India's SSI/SME Policy: Evolution and Growth

Since India's Independence, policymakers have adopted a dual strategy for SME (earlier VSI and latter SSI) promotion: (i) institutional infrastructure, and (ii) policy programmes. Broadly, SME policy evolution can be divided into three different phases:

- I Phase: Pre-liberalization period (1947-48 to 1990-91).
- II Phase: Liberalization period (1990-91 to 2005-06).
- III Phase: Liberalization period (2005-06 onwards).

Origin and I Phase (1947-48 to 1990-91): The origin of

India's SSI policy can be traced back to IPR, 1948 and IPR, 1956, both of which laid an exclusive emphasis on the promotion of modern small-scale industries as a major plank of India's economic development strategy. Accordingly, Small Industries Development Organization (SIDO) was established as an apex body for creating an exclusive institutional infrastructure at the national, state and district levels for SSI promotion. With the setting up of Village and Small Industries (VSI) Committee under the Chairmanship of D.G. Karve and with its recommendations, an exclusive protective framework for SSI promotion started emerging in the country (Kulkarni, 1991). Thus, both institutional infrastructure and protective policies were strengthened gradually and steadily from 1950s/1960s to late 1980s. This marked the first phase in the evolution of India's SSI policy characterized by both promotion and protection.

India's SSI Policy: II Phase (1990-91 to 2005-06): With the introduction of economic liberalization, Government of India brought out an exclusive SSI policy in August 1991, which indicated a shift in policy emphasis from protection to promotion of competitiveness (Ministry of Industry, 1991). This shift was reflected in two developments (Bala Subrahmanya, 1998):

1. Diluting market impediments and protection, and
2. Enhancing competitiveness of the sector.

The dilution of protective measures was characterized by abolishment of concessional finance, scaling down of fiscal incentives to confine to excise duty exemptions, a drastic reduction in the list of reserved items for exclusive SSI manufacturing (from about 850 to about 20), nullification of: (i) preferential access to imported raw materials and intermediates due to trade liberalization, and (ii) advantages available out of exemption from industrial licensing (IL) due to industrial de-licensing.

To promote competitiveness of the sector, institutional-cum-policy support was extended to overcome deficiencies with respect to technology, finance and market, among others. An exclusive Small Industries Development Bank of India (SIDBI) was created in 1990 with its branches in all State capitals. Equity participation by large firms up to 24 percent was introduced, to facilitate greater capital flow and modernization through inter-firm linkages. An exclusive Technology Bureau was created in 1995 to enable small firms to overcome technological obsolescence. In addition, technology information centres were set up in 1995. To promote inter-firm relationship between SSI and large firms, sub-contracting exchanges were set up through industry associations.

An exclusive Technology Development and Modernization Fund was set up in the same year. To promote quality consciousness and quality certification, financial support to acquire quality certifications was introduced. To promote internationalization through exports, a Market Development Assistance scheme was introduced in 2000. To facilitate collateral free loans to the sector, Credit Guarantee Fund Scheme was introduced, whereas efforts for technology upgradation were strengthened by initiating a credit linked capital subsidy scheme in 2000. Both dilution of protection and promotion of competitiveness continued till the promulgation of MSMED Act, 2006. This marked the end of second phase and the beginning of third phase in the evolution of India's SSI/SME policy.

India's SME Policy: III Phase (2005-06 onwards): The promulgation of Micro, Small and Medium Enterprises Development (MSMED) Act, 2006 marked a major milestone in the development of SME sector in India. With this Act, one of the long felt needs of this segment of the Indian economy was met. The MSMED Act, 2006 is unique for three important reasons:

1. The Act formally defined a medium scale enterprise for the first time in Indian economy,
2. The Act clubbed manufacturing and service sector enterprises together under one roof for common treatment and promotion, and

3. The Act raised the investment limit for manufacturing SSI by multiple (five) times.

This has resulted in India's graduation of its plank of small enterprise promotion from SSIs to SMEs, which is commonly followed in the global context.

Since the MSMED Act, 2006, the policymakers have exclusively focused on enhancing the competitiveness of the sector by periodic policy push in different forms, such as:

1. National Strategy for Manufacturing by NMCC (2006).
2. A promotional package for Micro and Small Enterprises (MSEs) (2007).
3. Facilitating early corporatization of SMEs through:
   - Removal of the restrictive ceiling of 24 percent for equity participation by other industrial enterprises, domestic or foreign, in MSEs.
   - Promulgation of Limited Liability Act, 2008.
4. Prime Minister's Task Force to address the issues of SMEs (2009).
5. National Manufacturing Policy (2011).
6. Twelfth Five Year Plan Working Group on MSMEs Growth (2012-2017).
7. Creation of SME Platforms in Bombay Stock Exchange (BSE) and National Stock Exchange (NSE) (2012).
8. Inter-Ministerial Committee for boosting exports of the MSME Sector (2013).
9. Inter-Ministerial Committee for Accelerating Manufacturing in the MSME Sector (2013).
10. Report on Financial Architecture for MSMEs (2015).
11. Framework for Revival and Rehabilitation of MSMEs (2015).
12. ASPIRE: A Scheme for Promotion of Innovation, Rural Industry and Entrepreneurship (2015).

All these policy initiatives have broadly aimed at lending inherent strength to the SME sector by tackling or overcoming obstacles in different functional areas such as finance, marketing, production technology and innovation, human resources, entrepreneurship, etc., among others. The objective is to achieve a qualitative shift in the development of a healthy and robust SME sector in the country. Thus, one can visualize three distinct phases in the evolution of India's SSI-cum-SME Policy over a period of time.

Growth Performance of SSIs (1990-91 to 2005-06) and SMEs (2005-06 to 2014-15) in India

Today, India's SME sector comprises three distinct segments within, which are as follows (Bala Subrahmanya, 2015a):

- Traditional industries and services promoted by livelihood based entrepreneurship,
- Modern industries and services promoted by policy induced entrepreneurship, and
- Knowledge based industries and services promoted by technology/innovation led entrepreneurship.

However, the focus of policy emphasis and therefore growth analysis is confined to modern industries and services comprising manufacturing and service industry enterprises, for the period from 1990-91 to 2014-15. In fact, up to 2005-06, SSIs predominantly comprised manufacturing enterprises whereas since 2005-06, SMEs consist of both manufacturing and service enterprises. Given this, the growth of SMEs relative to the growth of SSIs can be viewed in three different ways, as follows:

1. The shift in the size of units, employment, production and exports of SMEs in 2006-07 relative to that of SSI in 2005-06.
2. The average growth of SME units, employment, production and exports during 2006-07 to 2014-15 relative to that of SSI during 1990-91 to 2005-06.
3. Is there any trend in the growth performance of SSI and that of SMEs and whether the two are distinctly different? If yes, which one is better?

With the addition of small-scale service enterprises on the

one hand, and medium (manufacturing and service) enterprises on the other, the size of SMEs (relative to that of SSI) almost tripled in terms of units and production, but increased less than proportionately in terms of employment whereas increased only marginally in terms of exports. This can be attributed to the following factors:

1. In general, India's GDP growth is driven by service sector more than that of industry and agriculture. The number of service enterprises is much more than that of manufacturing enterprises even in the SME domain. Therefore, the addition of service enterprises led to a three-fold increase in the number of units.
2. However, increase in employment was not proportionate with that of units. This is because, single owner-cum-employee enterprises are quite common in the service sector across the world and so are in India. Therefore, their addition led to a less than proportionate increase in employment compared to that of units.
3. The increase in production was more than that of units. This could have emerged from medium (manufacturing and service) enterprises, which would have generated larger scale of output, relative to units and employment.
4. The marginal increase in exports could be due to exclusive/larger domestic market focus of service SMEs and medium manufacturing enterprises.

Given the above, it is appropriate to examine the growth pattern of SMEs relative to that of SSIs in terms of units, employment, production and exports. Table 2.1 presents the growth rate figures for SSIs and SMEs for units, employment, production and exports. SME performance was better than that of SSIs in terms of units, employment and production whereas it was marginally lower for exports.

Future Prospects and Policy Imperatives

The globalization of production has reached an unprecedented extent, with the production of goods and services increasingly fragmented across enterprises and countries. If MNCs of developed countries clearly lead this process, SMEs—their traditional partners as suppliers or distributors—are confronted by the diverse opportunities and challenges that arise from the new production context (OECD, 2008). Indian SMEs have to cope with these increasing trends of globalization in the future, and therefore enhancing their competitiveness is imperative. The current policy in terms of direction and emphasis is therefore welcome. However, it is important not to view the SME sector as one homogenous segment of the Indian economy. A conscious attempt must be made to separate "men from boys".

Table 2.1: Growth of SSIs (1990-91 to 2005-06) and SMEs (2006-07 to 2014-15)

Sector/Period	Units	Employment	Production	Exports
SSI: 1990-91 to 2005-06	4.06	4.23	4.26	12.53
SMEs: 2006-07 to 2014-15	4.40	4.80	7.11	11.93

Notes: (i) Growth of production is for the period 2006-07 to 2012-13 (at 2004-05 prices); (ii) Growth of exports is for the period 2006-07 to 2015-16 (in constant US$).
Source: Ministry of MSMEs, GoI.

Indian SME sector comprises of two sub-sectors: (i) the registered sector, and (ii) the unregistered sector. The unregistered sector SMEs are numerically significant as it accounted for 94 percent of the total SMEs whereas the remaining 6 percent SMEs constituted the registered sector (GoI, 2010). The unregistered sector would include predominantly, micro enterprises, largely located in rural India, with less educated entrepreneurs from poor income households, operating with outdated technology, limited access to institutional finance, and limited marketing/management expertise. The registered sector would predominantly consist of registered factory enterprises, mostly in urban and semi-urban areas, with better educated entrepreneurs from middle and higher income households, operating with relatively modern/sophisticated technology, better access to institutional finance, and with better marketing/management expertise.

Unregistered enterprises have only a transitional role in the process of economic development (Anderson, 1982). However, in underdeveloped countries like India, they grow much faster than they transform, in the absence of alternative employment opportunities (Bala Subrahmanya, 2015a). Entrepreneurship for unregistered enterprises emerges from less educated persons from low-income households in the form of household industries or unregistered workshops. In most cases, they cater to the needs of local demand, using local skills, local labour and local resources. Their primary objective in most cases is mere sustenance of their business and livelihood subsistence. Further, for many unregistered enterprises, the decision to remain informal (unregistered) may be deliberate, because the costs and procedural burden of joining the formal (registered) sector outweigh the benefits of staying in the informal (unregistered) sector (WBCSD, 2004).

However, if an entrepreneur of an unregistered enterprise is ambitious and able to achieve better economic performance successively, he/she is likely to transform his/her enterprise into a registered enterprise through scale expansion/technology modernization. In rural India, employees of unregistered workshops or children from household industries initiate an altogether new enterprise in the registered sector (for example, an employee of a bakery starts his own mechanized bakery, a timber merchant's son or employee starts his own saw mill, and an oil merchant's son starts his own oil mill) (Bala Subrahmanya, 1993).

Given the above, there are two important challenges that policy makers would confront on the development front of SMEs in India in the context of industrial development in the long-run (Bala Subrahmanya, 2014a):

1. How to transform the huge unregistered SMEs into the

registered SMEs?, and

2. How to enhance the competitiveness of the overall registered SME sector?

A substantial percentage of unregistered enterprises are local-market based, making use of local resources and local skills. Therefore, they will be looking for financial support more than anything else. Given this, it would be appropriate to undertake policy measures to set up exclusive "micro finance institutions" for "micro enterprise financing" to provide them timely and adequate finance. This would contribute to their sustenance and if they are successful, would enable them to transform eventually. Thus, the twin objectives in the context of unregistered SMEs are to enable them to either sustain or transform. Given this, the following policy initiatives will be beneficial:

1. The initiative of setting up MUDRA Bank is a welcome development in this regard. Efforts must be made to monitor the performance of MUDRA banks periodically, in terms of financial assistance flow to unregistered enterprises.
2. In addition, exclusive financial support for their expansion or scaling up may be provided through SSI branches of banks or SFCs or SIDBI.
3. The technical officers of District Industries Centres (DICs) should be trained to provide mentorship to unregistered enterprises at the district level.

The primary focus of policy machinery must be on the registered sector for competitiveness enhancement. The current focus on the sector to strengthen its competence in the functional areas (finance, HR, marketing, production and operations), simplifying bureaucratic procedures for its day-to-day operations, and lending support for quality improvement is welcome. In addition, an exclusive thrust must be laid on technological innovation promotion in the sector as a whole, particularly manufacturing SMEs. In fact, technological innovation is considered a key factor in a firm's competitiveness and it is unavoidable for firms which want to develop and maintain a competitive advantage and/or gain entry into new markets (Becheikh, et al., 2006). Technological innovation is a means to productivity growth (Zemplinerova and Hromadkova, 2012). It can be a critical driver for increasing productivity and competitiveness (Council on Competitiveness, 1999). Technological innovation has enabled Bangalore SMEs to grow faster (Bala Subrahmanya, 2015b).

However, in general, SMEs are identified with internal constraints to initiate and carry out innovations individually, due to inadequate firm level resources (Bala Subrahmanya, 2013a). Therefore, providing accessible external support is crucial. External support can play a decisive role in overcoming their isolation, and the economies of scale. External support can emerge in different forms of cooperation between firms of varying sizes—vertical and/or horizontal, among others—which can raise the competitive potential of SMEs through synergies and collective efficiencies, which individual producers can never attain alone (UNCTAD, 2005). Vertical linkages are to be nurtured between SMEs and their customers/suppliers or both, which are usually large firms. Horizontal linkages are to be cultivated among SMEs of the same sector or with government promoted SME technology centres or with academic institutions.

Cooperation with partners—upstream and downstream—improves SMEs' efficiency. This is due to the substantial benefits in terms of information flow, technology transfer and learning opportunities. There is evidence to confirm that the exposure of SMEs to learning processes among partners (involving MNCs) in global value chains generates knowledge spill-overs and stimulates human and technological capital upgrading (OECD, 2008). MNCs are central to global innovation patterns, and pivotal in the global value chains at the heart of international trade and investment nexus. This makes them potential sources of technology, know-how and good practices to support productivity growth in local SMEs and economies (UNCTAD, 2016).

Innovating and keeping up with new technologies are seen by SMEs as a requirement for their successful participation in global value chains (OECD, 2008).

Further, participation in global value chains enhances SME internationalisation and growth. It provides SME suppliers, access to global markets at lower costs than those faced by individual SMEs, due to the intermediation function assured by the contractor (MNCs). Firms that have successfully integrated into one or more value chains have been able to expand their business, and gain stability (OECD, 2008).

Inter-firm linkages between SMEs and large firms in India were found to be on the rise in the early 2000s (Bala Subrahmanya, 2014a). This is so despite the abolishment of Phased Manufacturing Programme (PMP) in the mid-1990s (Bala Subrahmanya, 2009). In fact, time is ripe to strongly promote inter-linkages of SMEs with other stakeholders comprising industry, government and academia, among others, due to the following developments.

National Level

- There has been a significant increase in the number of sub-contracting exchanges (SCXs) from a mere 35 (in SISIs) in the early 1990s to 86 (including 51 SCXs set up by Industry Associations/NGOs) by 2004 (Ministry of MSMEs, 2017a).
- A turnaround in the overall financial performance of PSUs and an increase in the proportion of profit making PSUs since 1990-91 (Bala Subrahmanya, 2014a). PSUs are major customers of SMEs, due to reservation of SSI products for exclusive public sector procurement, and price preference schemes.
- The penetration of MNCs (through FDI) into not only Tier I cities but also Tier II and Tier III cities, thereby generating scope for linkages between SMEs and MNCs in sub-urban and rural regions of India (NCAER, 2009).

International Level

- A steady increase of FDI in manufacturing (from US$ 135 billion in 2012 to US$ 388 billion in 2015), which in turn, is aided by M&A sales of MNCs (UNCTAD, 2016).
- A steady increase of FDI in services (from US$ 147 billion in 2012 to US$ 302 billion in 2015), which in turn, is aided by a rapid expansion of transportation and storage, and retail trade (the latter through the entry of MNC super market chains) into emerging/developing economies (UNCTAD, 2016).

Inter-firm/institution linkages have a strong influence on innovation, on the one hand, and internationalization, on the other (OECD, 2008). This has been recently substantiated in the context of India as well (Bala Subrahmanya, 2013a; Bala Subrahmanya, 2013b). All these have a positive influence on the economic performance and competitiveness of SMEs.

The current initiative of the government to promote "virtual clusters" to bring together SMEs, academic institutions, industry specific consultants, financial institutions, and various government departments, among others, to connect all stakeholders at one common platform is a welcome step in this direction (Ministry of MSMEs, 2017b). This will facilitate the promotion of both vertical and horizontal linkages of SMEs. However, something more needs to be done in this direction.

Horizontal linkages should be promoted as a means of promoting vertical linkages to enable Indian SMEs to join global value chains. To promote horizontal linkages, the following measures are recommended.

Triple helix interactions involving government, industry and academia should be promoted by bringing together SMEs, engineering education institutions, and DICs at the district level. Currently, there are more than 5,000 engineering educational institutions in the country promoted primarily by the private sector followed by the government and public-private-partnerships, offering under-graduate, post-graduate and/or diploma programmes (Career360, 2017). The state and district-wide network of engineering educational institutions across the country should be facilitated to link with local SMEs through collaborative work for innovations, with DICs as catalysts. Particularly, engineering student projects should be linked to local SME technical problems for ascertaining solutions. This would mutually contribute to the upgradation of quality. This exposure might even encourage innovative entrepreneurship for technology based start-ups, from the engineering institutions (Bala Subrahmanya, 2014b).

DICs must be well-equipped to act as catalysts, with a group of exclusively trained "techno-managerial officers" to forge links between SMEs and engineering institutions. The promotion and performance of industry-institute interactions must be monitored on a regular basis, and DICs must showcase better performers at the state and national level. This would spontaneously enable SMEs to develop vertical linkages with large firms including MNCs. The promotion of horizontal and vertical linkages would enable SMEs to innovate and internationalize, and thereby steadily achieve a higher economic performance. Even if, 10 percent of about 350 districts of India respond positively to this initiative, the much needed change would begin to occur for the benefit of the SME sector and thereby for India's economic development.

Summary and Conclusions

SMEs occupy an important role globally and more so in India. SMEs (earlier known as VSI and later as SSIs) have occupied a place of strategic significance in Indian economy ever since its Independence in 1947. The policymakers have recognized the role and importance of promoting the sector since IPR, 1948 and IPR, 1956. The major challenge immediately after Independence was to promote the growth of modern SSIs. Accordingly, a country-wide institutional network was developed over a period of time supplemented by a set of protective and promotional policy measures. However, with the initiation of economic liberalization in 1991, an exclusive SSI policy was introduced followed by a dilution of protective measures and strengthening of promotional measures. Since the promulgation of MSMED Act, 2006, policy emphasis has been consistently on the enhancement of SME competitiveness through the introduction of more and more policy measures.

Though on an average, SME growth performance during 2006-07 to 2014-15 was better than that of SSIs during 1990-91 to 2005-06, the positive growth trend has been consistent and significant only in terms of units and employment but not in terms of production and exports. This was largely attributed to the increasing dependence of SME production on the export market. The fluctuations in the international market have led to fluctuations in SME exports and thereby SME production. How to ensure a steady growth of SME production and exports in the international market is a major challenge? With the ever increasing trends of globalization, where production of goods and services are fragmented between firms of varying sizes across the world, the only option is to enhance the competitiveness of SMEs to increasingly penetrate the global market.

If SME competitiveness has to be steadily enhanced, the policy focus must be predominantly on the registered SMEs, to promote their vertical as well as horizontal linkages. Ideally, horizontal linkages should be promoted by means of triple helix interactions between government, industry and academia to network SMEs with engineering educational institutions at the district level, with DICs acting as the catalysts. This will be mutually beneficial for quality improvement. This would lead SMEs to develop vertical linkages with large firms including the MNCs. The promotion of horizontal and vertical linkages would enable SMEs to innovate and internationalize, and thereby achieve a higher economic performance. The resultant growth will be more steady and consistent, for the benefit of the sector as well as the economy.

References

Anderson, D. (1982), "Small Industry in Developing Countries:

Some Issues", World Bank Staff Working Papers, No. 518, Washington, D.C.

Bailetti, T. (2012), "Technology Entrepreneurship: Overview, Definition and Distinctive Aspects", *Technology Innovation Management Review*, February, pp. 5-12.

Bala Subrahmanya, M.H. (forthcoming), "Graduation from SSIs to SMEs in India: Policies, Performance and Challenges", *International Journal of Entrepreneurship and Small Business*, Inderscience Journal, UK.

——(2015a), "New Generation Start-Ups in India: What Lessons Can We Learn from the Past?", *Economic and Political weekly*, Volume L, No.12, pp. 56-63.

——(2015b), "Innovation and Growth of Engineering SMEs in Bangalore: Why Do Only Some Innovate and Only Some Grow Faster?", *Journal of Engineering and Technology Management*, Volume 36, pp. 24-40.

——(2014a), "Small-scale Industrialization under Globalization: Is the Tide Turning Around?", in Uma Kapila (ed.), 'Indian Economy since Independence', 25th edition, Academic Foundation, New Delhi.

——(2014b), "Technological Innovation in Manufacturing SMEs: A Decisive Means of Competitiveness", *Yojana*, Ministry of Information and Broadcasting, Government of India, New Delhi, Volume 58, November, pp. 4-9.

——(2013a), "External Support, Innovation and Economic Performance: What Firm Level Factors Matter for High-tech SMEs? and How?", *International Journal of Innovation Management*, Volume 17, pp. 1-26.

——(2013b), "Internationalization Motivation, Pattern and Process of Indian SMEs: Why? How? How Fast?", paper presented at the Workshop on Internationalization of Business Groups: Illustrations from China and India, December 5-6, 2013, National University of Singapore.

——(2009), "Industrial Policy and Management", ISTE-WPLP Learning Material Series, Indian Society for Technical Education, Working Professionals Learning Project, Bangalore.

——(1998), "Shifts in India's Small Industry Policy", *Small Enterprise Development,* Volume 9, Number 1, March, pp. 35-45.

——(1993), "Economics of Rural Industries in Karnataka", Ph.D.

thesis, Institute for Social and Economic Change, Bangalore.

Becheikh, N., R. Landry, and N. Amara (2006), "Lessons from Innovation Empirical Studies in the Manufacturing Sector: A Systematic Review of the Literature from 1993-2003", *Technovation*, Volume 26, Nos. 5-6, pp. 644-664.

Council on Competitiveness (1999), "The New Challenges to America's Prosperity: Findings from the Innovation Index", Washington, D.C.

Dalberg (2011), "Report on Support to SMEs in Developing Countries through Financial Intermediaries", Dalberg Global Development Advisors, Geneva.

DCSSI (1985), "Annual Report: 1984-85", Government of India, New Delhi.

Government of India (2010), "Report of the Prime Minister's Task Force on Micro, Small and Medium Enterprises", New Delhi.

Kulkarni, M.R. (1991), "Industrial Development", Third Edition, National Book Trust, India, New Delhi.

Kushnir, K., M.L. Mirmulstein and R. Ramalho (2010), "Micro, Small, and Medium Enterprises around the World: How Many Are There, and What Affects the Count?", The World Bank and International Finance Corporation, Washington D.C.

Ministry of Commerce and Industry (2011), "National Manufacturing Policy 2011", Government of India, New Delhi.

Ministry of Industry (1991), "Policy Measures for Promoting and Strengthening Small, Tiny and Village Enterprises", Government of India, New Delhi.

Ministry of MSMEs (2017a), "Subcontracting Exchanges for Ancillary Development", available at: http://www.dcmsme.gov.in/schemes/sccontexc.htm.

Ministry of MSMEs (2017b), "MSME Virtual Clusters", available at: http://msmevirtualclusters.in/home.aspx.

Ministry of MSMEs (2016), "Annual Report: 2015-16", Government of India, New Delhi.

Ministry of MSMEs (2013), "Recommendations of the Inter-Ministerial Committee for Accelerating Manufacturing in Micro, Small and Medium Enterprises Sector", Government of India, New Delhi.

Ministry of MSMEs (2012), "Report of the Working Group on Micro, Small and Medium Enterprises (MSMEs) Growth for 12th Five Year Plan (2012-2017)", Government of India, New

Delhi.

Ministry of MSMEs (2010), "Micro, Small and Medium Enterprises in India: An Overview", Government of India, New Delhi.

NCAER (2009), "FDI in India and its Growth Linkages", Study Report, New Delhi.

OECD (2008), "Enhancing the Role of SMEs in Global Value Chains", OECD Centre for Entrepreneurship, SMEs and Local Development, Paris.

RBI (2017), "Handbook of Statistics on Indian Economy", Reserve Bank of India, Mumbai.

SBA Office of Advocacy (2014), "Frequently Asked Questions: Advocacy: The Voice of Small Business in Government", available at: https://www.sba.gov/sites/default/files/FAQ_March_2014_0.pdf.

UNCTAD (2016), "World Investment Report, 2016", Geneva.

UNCTAD (2005), "How to Build an Effective Policy Framework for SMEs: A Developing Countries' Perspective", paper presented at the International Conference on reforming the Business Environment, Cairo, Egypt, November 29-December 1.

WBCSD (2004), "Promoting Small and Medium Enterprises for Sustainable Development", World Business Council for Sustainable Development, Geneva.

Zemplinerova, A. and E. Hromadkova (2012), "Determinants of Firm's Innovation", *Prague Economic Papers*, Volume 4, pp. 487-502.

3

MSMEs in India: Challenges of Informality and Globalization

Keshab Das

The Context

The survival, growth and decline of manufacturing enterprises, wherever and of whatever size, have almost always occurred in response to the opportunities provided by or, lost mainly due to two crucial factors, changes in market conditions and technological advancements. For the enterprises, responding to these two factors comprise their major challenges in retaining or changing their characteristics relating to scale or size of operations. There has also been the exogenous factor of policies that buttress or constrain the growth and survival of firms.

The industrial base of India, a labour surplus and vast domestic market-based economy, has been marked by the preponderance of micro, small and medium enterprises (MSMEs) which have dominated in terms of number of units, employment, product types and regional spread. There has been no relenting in the growth of these enterprises over the decades at least since the early 1980s. The sustained rise in the number of MSMEs defies the proposition made by Anderson (1982) that micro and small firms would essentially clear the industrial space either by moving up in the scale or, eventually, *withering away*, as these would be rendered inefficient while competing with their larger counterparts. In fact, the MSMEs have emerged both resilient and dynamic in accommodating workers with diverse skill levels (including the unskilled ones) and catering to the myriad forms of demand as emerges in a calibrated income distribution context—spanning local to global.

The rise and spread of MSMEs signal their growing relevance in an unequally endowed economy whereby these have contributed immensely over the decades in generating opportunities in local employment and income. While engaged in the manufacturing of over 8,000 products, this huge sector often draws its resources—raw materials and human—locally and caters to a calibrated demand extending from local to global. This also implies that MSMEs have been contributing towards keeping regional disparities in check by dissuading desperate migration in search of employment elsewhere. There have been several industrial sub-sectors wherein MSMEs have displayed competence in terms of product quality and efficiency through innovative activities and also being responsive to demand-side requirements. In this process, such MSMEs have also played a catalytic role for others in the sector or region to emulate and excel.

Though still on a relatively limited scale, several MSMEs have not only been making efforts towards upgrading product quality by introducing alternative raw materials and new processes but also by introducing organisational/management changes in order to respond to the requirements of global buyers or niche markets abroad. With the deepening of the engagement of Indian MSMEs with global buyers, often forming part of a preferred conduit of bilateral trade and investment agreements, global production networks (GPNs) have been influencing existing forms of organisation of production. Efforts in this direction of participating on a greater scale in the global market space have also brought up several new challenges to the local firms in responding to the complexities of complying with both product and process standards.

Interestingly, as globalization tendencies deepen in India, MSMEs have come to capture the imagination of policymakers, development practitioners and global buyers not merely due to their continuing contribution to local economic regeneration and export earnings, but also because of a unique ability to be responsive to changes in the spheres of market and innovation—domestic or global. An impressive repertoire of small firm development policy notwithstanding, this sector's performance during the economic reforms period, which has over emphasized external orientation, has been particularly worrisome. The overwhelming presence of informality in both the production and labour processes has serious implications for sustainable business as well as competitiveness.

This paper addresses some of these important concerns of MSMEs from a policy perspective and deals with structural constraints as a deep-seated informality in both the production and labour processes. Some of the concerns include constraints in accessing loan finance and business services, poor innovation resulting in sub-standard product quality, prevalence of the low-road syndrome in industrial clusters and, importantly, neglect of the safety and social security aspects of labour. Discussions include challenges confronted by Indian MSMEs in the process of participating in the global market arena whether through global production networks or as direct exporters.

Definitional and Database Issues

So far as the official statistics are concerned, in India, MSMEs have been defined based on a unique parameter, namely, historical value of an enterprise's investment in plant and machinery. This is, possibly, the most unusual variable ever followed in any other nation where employment size and/or annual turnover are typically used as indicators to classify enterprises by size; a fairly detailed compilation of different criteria followed by countries across the globe is presented in Das (2011a: 4-6). Albeit on several occasions a shift towards a *universal* approach to defining MSEs/MSMEs has been debated in the policy circles and representations made by national level apex small enterprise associations, there have been very little move towards a radical shift.

What, however, has been worked upon concerns rounds of changes in the ceiling (of investment in plant and machinery) specifications and introduction of a few *new* categories of enterprises within MSMEs such as based on the primary nature of transactions carried out by the firms. Table 3.1 brings together information on changes in definition and introduction of various categories of MSMEs since the 1980s.

Table 3.1: Criteria of Defining and Creation of New Categories of MSMEs in India: 1980 to 2006

Year	Manufacturing Enterprises					Enterprises Providing Services		
	Upper limit of the historical/original value of plant and machinery (₹ million)					Upper limit of the investment in equipments (₹ million)		
	M	S	A	Tiny*/Micro	EOU	M	S**	Micro
1980	-	2.0	2.5	0.2	-	-	-	-
1985	-	3.5	4.5	0.2	-	-	0.2	-
1991	-	6.0	7.5	0.5	7.5	-	0.5	-
1997	-	30.0	30.0	2.5	30.0	-	0.5	-
1999	-	10.0	10.0	2.5	10.0	-	0.5	-
2001	-	10.0***	10.0	2.5	10.0	-	1.0	-
2006	100.0	50.0	10.0	2.5	10.0	50.0	20.0	1.0

M = Medium; S = Small; A = Ancillary

Notes: '-' indicates never defined, formally.

EOU: Export Oriented Unit; this category was introduced in 1991.

*In 1980, these referred to the units located in rural areas or towns having a maximum population of 50,000 as per *Census of India, 1971*. By 1985, the population limit increased to 0.5 million as per *Census of India, 1981*. However, by 1991, the locational conditions had been dropped.

**SSSE: Small Scale Service Establishment; introduced in 1985.

SSSBE: Small Scale Service and Business Enterprise; this category replaced SSSE since 1991.

***Since October 2001, for 41 items of hosiery and hand tools; since June 2003, for 23 more items of stationery and drugs and pharmaceutical industry and since October 2004 for 7 more items of sports goods the upper limit of investment had been raised to ₹ 50 million.

Source: Das (2011b: 5).

A close look at the varying criteria (or investment ceiling) over the years suggest that the limits for micro and small manufacturing enterprises have leapt at certain intervals of time, but more so during the post-reforms period. While these affirmed a growing policy emphasis on relatively larger enterprises, one notices the inclusion of the so-called export oriented units (EOUs) suggesting preference for external orientation by MSMEs. The most significant dimension of definitional changes has, obviously, been the introduction of the 'medium' enterprise category through the Micro, Small and Medium Enterprises Development (MSMED) Act of 2006. Although the 'medium' enterprise size has been a globally recognized one for long, its inclusion in the Indian policy domain reiterated the important role expected to be played by the larger enterprises so far as competitiveness in the global market sphere is concerned. The formal inclusion of the medium category, in a sense, acknowledged the gradual maturing of SMEs, both technologically and organizationally, at least in certain modern sub-sectors.

While the policy bias towards relatively larger and export oriented firms could be discernible during the post-reforms period, it is important to observe that official statistics would clearly show the massive presence of micro enterprises within the MSMEs. In fact, despite concerns in comparability, the four national *Censuses* of SSIs/MSMEs (held for the years 1972, 1987-88, 2001-02 and 2006-07) so far unequivocally established the growing incidence of micro enterprises which mostly belonged to the unorganized sector (typically over 80 percent of all enterprises) and above half of these units are located in rural areas or what are called 'village towns'. For instance, as per the latest (2006-07) MSME *Census*, the unorganized units accounted for a staggering 94 percent of all enterprises and 52 percent of all units were rural based (Das, 2014: 58). The deep-seated informality in MSMEs, hence, is an issue that cannot be washed away as an unimportant or transient phenomenon, from the policy perspective at the least.

Growth and Performance of the Sector

The growth and performance of the MSMEs during the post-reforms period have been impressive, going by the statistics as provided in the successive annual reports of the concerned ministry. However, given the number of problems associated with the data provided, one needs to be careful in deciphering the numbers and trends. It is not possible to compare the data between the pre-MSMED Act, 2006 and the one following that, as disaggregated data have been unavailable in the public domain. Further, it is amply clear that much of these official data might be difficult to accept as being reliable. For instance, (and as has been pointed out on several earlier occasions, as in Das, 2008a), the growth rate of the number of units during a fairly long period (1990-2006) has remained fixed at the *providential* figure of 4.07 percent. The issue of performance of the MSME sector remains clouded under the fact that *sickness* of enterprises is hardly highlighted in the annual reports of the ministry.

Given the state of database, Tables 3.2 and 3.3 report official statistics as made available. It is obvious that on all counts—number of enterprises, employment and value of output—that during the post-reforms period, this sector has witnessed positive changes as all these variables show a steady growth over the years. The data quality deficiency notwithstanding, it is important to note that the average size (employment per enterprise) of MSEs has remained at 2.4 all throughout the period 1990-2006, establishing the very small size of the enterprises which would seriously impact the efficiency and production capability of firms in the absence of any noticeable investment in technology. The very small average size, eventually, points to the overwhelmingly informal character of the Indian small firm sector. The disturbing issue is that while MSMEs are envisaged as sources of generating huge number of jobs across skills, the growth of labour productivity has dropped far below that of capital productivity. Further, the level and rate of output growth do not necessarily influence employment (Das, 2008a: 123-124).

Table 3.2: Aspects of Growth of MSEs in India: 1990-2006

Year	Total MSEs (in million)	Production (₹ million) Constant Prices*	Employment (in million)
1990-91	6.79	847280	15.83
1991-92	7.06 (4.07)	873550 (3.10)	16.60 (4.83)
1992-93	7.35 (4.07)	922460 (5.60)	17.48 (5.33)
1993-94	7.65 (4.07)	987960 (7.10)	18.26 (4.46)
1994-95	7.96 (4.07)	1087740 (10.10)	19.14 (4.79)
1995-96	8.28 (4.07)	1211750 (11.40)	19.79 (3.42)
1996-97	8.62 (4.07)	1348920 (11.32)	20.59 (4.00)
1997-98	8.97 (4.07)	1462629 (8.43)	21.32 (3.55)
1998-99	9.34 (4.07)	1575251 (7.70)	22.06 (3.46)
1999-00	9.72 (4.07)	1703792 (8.16)	22.91 (3.88)
2000-01	10.11 (4.07)	1844014 (8.23)	23.87 (4.21)
2001-02	10.52 (4.07)	1956130 (6.06)	24.93 (4.44)
2002-03	10.95 (4.07)	3067710 (8.68)	26.02 (4.36)
2003-04	11.40 (4.07)	3363440 (9.64)	27.14 (4.31)
2004-05	11.86 (4.07)	3729380 (10.88)	28.26 (4.11)
2005-06	12.34 (4.07)	4188840 (12.32)	29.99(4.44)

Notes: Figures in parentheses indicate percentage growth over the previous year.
* Up to 2001-02, figures are at 1993-94 prices, and beyond that at 2001-02 prices.
Source: Das (2011b: 7).

The performance of MSMEs in the export sphere has often been highlighted as a bright spot of the sector implying major improvements in the product quality and a rise in firm competitiveness. It is useful to examine the growth rate of value of exports (in USD terms) from this sector to have an idea about the export situation.

It is unclear if the contribution to exports came mostly from the medium enterprises since 2006-07. Data on exports from the MSME sector continues to remain incomprehensive as disaggregated statistics by size is not readily available. Similarly, it is difficult to indicate, particularly for the post-MSMED Act period, which products mostly composed the export basket. In fact, such data on product group-wise export value figures were available till 2007-08 with the Ministry of Industry on a regular basis and since then accessing data for subsequent years has been problematic.

Table 3.3: Aspects of Growth of MSMEs in India: 2006-2015

Year	Units (million nos.)	Production (₹ billion; constant prices)	Employment (million nos.)
2006-07	36.18	11988.18	80.52
2007-08	37.74	13229.60	84.20
2008-09	39.37	13756.99	88.08
2009-10	41.08	14883.90	92.18
2010-11	42.87	16555.81	96.52
2011-12	44.77	17908.05	101.18
2012-13	46.76	18099.76	106.15
2013-14	48.86		111.43
2014-15	51.06		117.13

Notes: From 2006-07, MSMEs include wholesale/retail trade, legal, educational and social services, hotels and restaurants, transport and storage and warehousing (except cold storage), data for which was extracted from *Economic Census, 2005.*
Production figures are at constant (2004-05) prices.
Source: RBI (2016).

In Table 3.4, data have been presented for the value of exports from the small enterprise sector for the two decade period of 1988-2008. It may be surmised from the table that there have hardly been any changes in the composition of product groups over the rather long period, except in the 'electronic and computer software' one. This is surprising as Indian small enterprises have been engaged in the production of a wide variety of items for which there would be a good demand worldwide.

Table 3.4: Exports of Major Product Groups from the Indian SSI Sector: 1988-2008

(value in ₹ million)

Product Group	1990-91*	2000-01	2007-08
Engineering goods	657.3 (8.7)	5956.4 (10.3)	39865.7 (22.4)
Readymade garments	3102.9 (40.9)	23473.5 (40.7)	35250.3 (19.8)
Electronic and computer software	-	1656.2 (2.9)	29109.6 (16.4)
Chemicals and allied products	90.4 (1.2)	510.3 (0.9)	19628.0 (11.0)
Processed foods	309.0 (4.1)	5620.1 (9.7)	16696.6 (9.4)
Basic chemicals, pharmaceuticals and cosmetics	1046.7 (13.8)	5756.7 (10.0)	7399.0 (4.2)
Finished leather and leather products	1559.9 (20.5)	3904.7 (6.8)	9595.0 (5.4)
Marine products	268.1 (3.5)	2055.9 (3.6)	6451.8 (3.6)
Plastics products	47.7 (0.6)	1213.1 (2.1)	3538.6 (2.0)
Cashew kernel, cashew nut shell liquid	316.6 (4.2)	1981.0 (3.4)	2427.1 (1.4)
Woollen garments and knitwear	84.5 (1.1)	2097.8 (3.6)	1939.4 (1.1)
Woollen garments and knitwear	84.5 (1.1)	2097.8 (3.6)	1939.4 (1.1)
Synthetic and rayon textiles	11.4 (0.2)	955.5 (1.7)	2393.8 (1.3)
Processed tobacco, snuff and bidis	16.4 (0.2)	637.9 (1.1)	1040.1 (0.6)
Spices, spice oil oleoresins	19.7 (0.3)	1504.6 (2.6)	906.5 (0.5)
Forest product	-	-	901.2 (0.5)
Sports goods	53.2 (0.7)	243.0 (0.4)	495.1 (0.3)
Lac product	16.5 (0.2)	93.1 (0.2)	148.0 (0.1)
Total	7600.3 (100.0)	58488.0 (100.0)	177785.6 (100.0)

Notes: Figures in brackets are respective column percentages.
* End-year of three yearly averages.
Sources: Das (2011b: 9) and GoI (2005 and 2009).

Even the respective shares have not changed very much over the 20-year period. Moreover, just about seven product groups (engineering goods, readymade garments, electronic and computer software, chemicals and allied products, processed foods, basic chemicals, pharmaceuticals and cosmetics, and finished leather and leather products) have, typically, accounted for close to 90 percent of the total value of exports from the small enterprises.

Limited Access to Formal Credit

Among several challenges facing Indian MSMEs, the most enduring one has been access to and availability of adequate loan finance on time. This is an issue which almost always finds mention in any reasonable discussion on the sector and remains a serious one particularly for the informal and micro enterprises across the country. Irrespective of policy initiatives and government pronouncements, as several studies have shown, MSEs continue to depend on non-formal sources of finance often with unfavourable repayment terms. As shown in Table 3.5, the share of small enterprises in gross bank credit had fallen almost till 2006-07 and there has been a rise since then. The situation has turned graver during the post-reforms period as the credit share of small enterprises from the formal banking sources has followed a declining trend—since then, economic reforms formally were pursued as a state macroeconomic strategy.

The more disturbing aspect of this credit squeeze is, in fact, a significant fall in similar loans available to such enterprises based in rural areas. It is important to reflect that the state has been unresponsive to the financial needs of MSEs even when these have been promised under the so-called priority sector lending, overseen by the Reserve Bank of India (RBI).

The pattern and extent of credit available to the MSMEs, as depicted through the official database of the RBI fails to reveal the magnitude and sources of loan finance for the informal enterprises, whether in rural or urban areas. The grave neglect that the informal enterprises have suffered over several decades concerning access to finance also reflects the crisis of the sector in terms of scaling up or building up the manufacturing competitiveness.

The provision of banks not to insist on collateral while considering a loan request has not quite been a catalyst in enhancing funds access by micro enterprises, especially, due mainly to their informal status which substantially discourages the bankers to take a 'risk' in approving the application.

Table 3.5: Small Enterprises' Share in Gross Bank Credit: 1990-2016

Year	SSIs/SEs (₹ billion)	SSIs/SEs Share of Gross Bank Credit (percent)
1990-91	179.38	29.1
1991-92	189.39	29.0
1992-93	209.75	26.7
1993-94	239.78	29.8
1994-95	291.75	28.5
1995-96	342.46	27.4
1996-97	381.96	27.6
1997-98	457.71	28.4
1998-99	516.79	28.9
1999-00	570.35	28.5
2000-01	601.41	27.5
2001-02	671.07	29.2
2002-03	647.07	21.9
2003-04	712.09	22.7
2004-05	834.98	19.7
2005-06	1012.85	18.4
2006-07	1273.23	18.3
2007-08	2135.39	24.9
2008-09	2561.28	24.3
2009-10	3622.91	27.6
2010-11	4785.27	29.8
2011-12	5276.84	27.2
2012-13	6872.08	30.8
2013-14	8510.92	33.8
2014-15	9611.74	36.2
2015-16	9957.12	36.5

Note: Small enterprises (SEs) replaced small-scale industries (SSIs) following the MSMED Act, 2006.

Source: Reserve Bank of India, *Handbook of Statistics on Indian Economy* (various issues).

This brings to the fore the relatively recent policy initiative of introducing the Micro Units Development and Refinance Agency (MUDRA) Bank scheme in 2015. The MUDRA scheme, essentially, targets the fund needs of micro enterprises with three size classes, namely, Shishu (loans up to ₹ 50,000), Kishor (loans from ₹ 50,000 to ₹ 5 lakh) and Tarun (loans above ₹ 5 lakh and up to ₹ 10 lakh). Based on the functional strategy of refinancing by SIDBI, the loans would be delivered through nationalised banks, primary lending institutions, NBFCs, MFIs, rural banks, district banks, private banks and other intermediaries. That this much-hyped scheme has hardly made any progress, especially, following the demonetization drive since November 2016, is being recognised by sector analysts; a discussion on the MUDRA initiative is presented in Nair and Das (2015).

The financing of MSEs in particular has been constrained by limited useful information on the enterprises which could form a reliable base for bankers to be confident about considering agreeing to a loan request. In fact, the disincentives that are embedded in offering a loan that is not repaid, acts as a barrier to facilitative financing of small firms by the formal banking system. Similarly, there have been few takers for the Credit Guarantee Scheme either because it is not widely known (and understood) or informal enterprises would not be covered under this initiative.

Infrastructure and Innovation: Areas of Concern

Even as the MSME sector has remained huge and varied, an area of much neglect has been what may be termed as business infrastructure. In fact, there has been a dearth of studies on this aspect of MSMEs in India. In a significant study on small enterprises covering about 12 states, detailed enquiries were made regarding the nature and extent of infrastructure constraints faced by individual entrepreneurs (Das and Morris, 2001: 205-227).

Of the several infrastructure related issues that were revealed through these primary field-based enquiries, it was clear that electricity, transportation (roads and railways), water and (in specific industries) and common effluent treatment plants (CETPs) were the most sought after provisions that restrained the potential of MSMEs. The policy neglect of these various components of infrastructure facilities for businesses continues to be an important lapse in upgrading this sector's contribution. Apart from these components of infrastructure, there have been concerns regarding enterprises' lack of awareness about various crucial business related information as, for instance, various official/administrative procedures in matters of exports, government concessions, skill up-gradation programmes, external markets, newer and better technologies and so on.

Poor provision of business infrastructure for the MSMEs is closely linked to the absence or inadequacy of innovation activities within the enterprises. In fact, the neglect of innovation is so palpable that there is hardly any comprehensive and periodic statistics showing investment in R&D at the enterprise level. This is in complete contrast to the fact of establishment of the National Manufacturing Competitiveness Council, the focus of which is building up of innovation activities at the enterprise level. As discussed in Das and Joseph (2014: 133-136), investment in in-house R&D has been one of the least important activities pursued by MSMEs in India. Similarly, unlike in several countries across the world, there is hardly any interaction between enterprises and the formal research systems as in universities or institutions; the state has also contributed little in facilitating such mutuality that could act as a catalyst to innovation activities in MSMEs. "While the available evidence, mostly from the developed world, indicates that interaction with universities and public research institutions (PRIs) is an important source of means of innovation in the manufacturing enterprises, in India, however, industry-university interaction is still in its infancy (Das and Joseph, 2014: 138).

What is worrying is not so much that there have been

limited PRIs to promote innovation and R&D for MSMEs in India; in fact, there have been a slew of such organisations catering to the MSMEs in general and also to specific sub-sectors for a broad range of services. For instance, the Technology Development Board provides for financial assistance in the form of equity, soft loans or grants, and there exists sub-sectoral (or, product-specific) PRIs in such goods as leather, gems, rubber, plastics. "The launch of technology business incubators in 2001, by the National Research Development Corporation, Bureau of Indian Standards, National Productivity Council, Consultancy Development Centre and Electronics Test and Design Centres are all part of the formal strategy to improve competitiveness of the SMEs" (Das, 2011a: 87).

Unless the local firms interact with the regional and local innovation systems, with a strong support by the state, it is unlikely that these firms would build their technological capabilities essential for competing abroad as also at home where large scale dumping of foreign, often Chinese, goods has dented the prospects of Indian MSMEs. That would imply that Indian MSMEs would benefit not just by sub-sectoral technology-centric institutional support but a variety of region specific business infrastructure must go alongside to render any such intervention in promoting innovation activities worthwhile.

A possibility in bringing together the strengths of infrastructure benefits and innovation facilitation at the enterprise level was purported to be carried out in the promotion of industrial clusters. Deeply influenced by the UNIDO Cluster Development Programme, the Indian state and non-state approach to industrial cluster promotion has been aiming to build up technological and organisational capabilities at least since the late 1990s or so. The detailed steps involved in implementing this sector-centric approach have been problematic as the initiative misses out on the *spatiality* of the cluster dynamics (Das, 2005). By overemphasizing aspects such as business development services and outward orientation, the substantive constraints as generic cluster specific infrastructure have been neglected. "All that these programmes have managed to highlight is the role of certain business development services, cluster development agents and, of late, a nonchalant approach to linking cluster development with poverty reduction" (Das, 2008b: 231). The truncated cluster development approach in India has been an important roadblock in up-gradation of MSMEs in manufacturing better quality products whether for the domestic or the global markets.

It may be reiterated that the absence of technological dynamism in industrial clusters has often been closely linked to the poor regional innovation systems and lack of basic infrastructure at the cluster level. "The very spatiality of clusters that suffers from the double whammy of poor infrastructural endowments of the region and absence of a formal innovation system ultimately reinforces exclusion" (Das, 2011c: 296). There are additional *soft* issues like inadequacy or non-existence of collective action by clustered enterprises as a strategy to achieve success in non-competitive areas. The strong presence of informality could act as a major disincentive to collectivity; the cluster intervention strategies need to recognise this important dimension.

External Orientation of MSMEs as Policy Fixation

As discussed earlier, decades of small enterprise policy structure notwithstanding the MSME sector, in general, and micro enterprises, in particular, have been severely constrained by limited access to credit, inadequacy of business infrastructure and a weak institutional framework not conducive to pursue a higher path of technological and innovation progress. Several decades of state protection has been manifest through such fiscal and other mechanisms as offering concessional duties/taxes, enhancing import tariffs, specifying product reservation, proposing targeted credit, restricting production capacity, imposing government procurement and providing for acquiring land and machinery by MSMEs at easy terms. It is possible to argue that many of these policy initiatives may have helped certain enterprises in certain sub-sectors. However, there have been studies which point to the weak or partial or biased implementation of these policies defeating the original purpose. That the informal enterprises were left out of such policy efforts and that often entrepreneurs were unaware of such facilities have been documented widely.

In any case, Indian MSMEs—with notable exceptions in specific sub-sectors and enterprises—continued to produce low quality goods and did not display impressive performance in the global market. However, with the MSMED Act, 2006, the government seemed obsessed with emphasizing external orientation of MSMEs to be an active participant in the global market. While the deepening neo-liberal tendencies helped consolidate the idea of market-supremacy, neo-localism also held its sway simultaneously, reiterating that the local enterprises would do well *only* by relating to the global buyers and consumers. With SMEs construed as a useful subject in trade negotiations, the globalisation imperatives dominated policy thinking. No wonder, all the following important government documents viz., Report of Prime Minister's Task Force on Micro, Small and Medium Enterprises, 2010; Recommendations of the Inter-Ministerial Committee for Accelerating Manufacturing in Micro, Small and Medium Enterprises Sector, 2013; and Report of the Inter-Ministerial Committee for Boosting Exports from MSME Sector, 2013, stressed the significance of external orientation of MSMEs as an important strategy of regional industrialisation. Amongst several policy approaches in this direction, it is possible to discern the following:

1. Recognizing the importance of 'medium' and 'business service' enterprises.
2. Enhancing competitiveness by focusing product quality

improvement as the key.

3. Networking with potential stakeholders with the aim to broad-base enterprise gains at the levels of the sector as well as local space.
4. Broadening or seeking larger market presence with the primary objective of exporting. Hence, towards promoting innovation, learning and market access for MSMEs, the post-reforms policy has emphasized the importance of internationalization for local firms.

A definitive route through which internationalization of local firms is made possible has been to participate in the global production networks (GPNs). While there have been contrasting claims as to if such a manner of linking to global buyers and consumers brings benefits of creating job opportunities and exposure of advanced technology and management practices to the local enterprises GPNs, there are certain sub-sectors—for instance, leather goods, gems and jewellery, apparels, engineering and auto parts, tea, pharmaceuticals and chemicals—where GPNs have been active but with Indian MSMEs acting as sub-contractors or job workers to global buyers who are, usually, transnational corporations (TNCs).

What is disturbing about such arrangements is that often these contracts lack transparency (Das, forthcoming). In fact, several of Indian MSMEs have participated in GPNs in such activities which involve low value addition and labour intensive and repetitive tasks whether in processing, assembling or manufacturing. The downside of such *asymmetrical relationships* between the TNCs and local producers has been well recognised (Knorringa and Meyer-Stamer, 2008: 30-34) compelling one to seriously rethink the mechanisms of such 'rent-poor' activities befalling on the producers from the developing economies. The perpetuation of what may be described as neo-imperialistic tendencies that subjugates MSMEs from developing economies to buyers from the global North, is a matter of much concern in such policy preference for GPNs as beneficial for local enterprises.

Beyond the problem of transparency of contracts, the GPNs have been exclusionary as only a miniscule of enterprises could actually be chosen by the TNCs to participate as sub-contractors. It has not been established yet that such working arrangement with a few could actually transform other non-participating units through indirect influences in conducting business. Moreover, it has been noted widely that the participating enterprises simultaneously produce for the domestic and low-end markets using the same manufacturing facility and compromising on both product and process standards. The GPN preoccupation also suggests that a large number of producers (or, MSMEs) not engaged in making such products which fall outside the interest of the global buyers would not be able to access certain business even as mere sub-contractors.

Concluding Observations

The role and contribution of MSMEs in economic development of a developing economy need no underscoring as these enterprises have been acting as sources of employment potential, catering to various market needs and regional economic regeneration. In the Indian context, from a policy point of view, MSMEs have been assigned a key role in local and regional economic progress. While the number and geographical spread of these enterprises have been quite impressive, two specific broad challenges have confronted the nature and direction of growth of MSMEs in India.

Characterised by high degree of informality, Indian MSMEs have often missed out on accessing a variety of supply-side advantages, prominent amongst them being loan finance from the formal sources. The other constraints, not connected to the informality conundrum, have been due to limits of business infrastructure and the concomitant possibility to engage in innovative activities. Given these weaknesses of policies, it is no surprise to observe that the rural enterprises have been the hardest hit.

This leads to the second broad challenge—that of surviving and growth in times of deepening of globalisation. At least since the economic reforms and liberalisation processes have been formally pursued as macro policy strategies, Indian MSMEs have been making efforts to respond to the imperatives of participating in the global production and business space. The policy changes during this phase do reflect the state's keenness to buttress external orientation of MSMEs through a variety of incentives and capacity building exercises. In this process, GPNs have received much fillip offering a larger scope to TNCs to engage MSMEs albeit in certain sub-sectors and 'tasks'. *Inter alia*, the terms of such international sub-contracting have often lacked transparency subjugating local producers to the *diktats* of the global buyer.

The discussions of these challenges strongly suggest a critical relook at policies to promote Indian MSMEs to emerge as dynamic, strong and socially relevant.

References

Anderson, Dennis (1982), "Small Industry in Developing Countries: A Discussion of Issues", *World Development*, 10(11).

Das, Keshab (2005), "Industrial Clustering in India: Local Dynamics and the Global Debate", in Keshab Das (ed.), 'Indian Industrial Clusters', Ashgate, Aldershot, UK.

Das, Keshab (2008a), "Micro, Small and Medium Enterprises: Unfair Fare", in Alternative Survey Group (ed.), 'Alternative Economic Survey, India 2007-2008: Decline of the Developmental State', Daanish Books, Delhi.

Das, Keshab (2008b), "Indian Small Firms Under Globalization: Has Policy Helped?", in Jerry Haar and Jörg Mayer-Stamer (eds.), 'Small Firms, Global Markets: Competitive Challenges in the New Economy', Palgrave Macmillan, Hampshire, UK.

Das, Keshab (2011a), "Small and Medium Enterprise (SME) Competitiveness: Issues and Initiatives", Gujarat Industrial Development Corporation, Gandhinagar.

Das, Keshab (2011b), "Indian Micro and Small Enterprises in a Changing Policy Environment", in Keshab Das (ed.), 'Micro and

Small Enterprises in India: The Era of Reforms', Routledge, New Delhi.

Das, Keshab (2011c), "Indian Rural Clusters and Innovation: Challenges for Inclusion", *Economics, Management, and Financial Markets*, 6(1).

Das, Keshab (2014), "Micro, Small and Medium Enterprises", in School of Social Sciences (ed.), 'Industrial Development in India: Boundary of Industry', (BECE-107, Block 2), Indira Gandhi National Open University, New Delhi.

Das, Keshab (forthcoming), "Situating Labour in the Global Production Network Debate: As if the 'South' Mattered", *The Indian Journal of Labour Economics*.

Das, Keshab and K.J. Joseph (2014), "On Learning, Innovation and Competence Building in India's SMEs: The Challenges Ahead", in Ana Arroio and Mario Scerri (eds.), 'The Promise of Small and Medium Enterprises', BRICS National Innovation Systems Series, Routledge, New Delhi.

Das, Keshab and Sebastian Morris (2001), "Infrastructural Constraint and Small Firms", in Morris, Sebastian, Rakesh Basant, Keshab Das, K. Ramachandran and Abraham Koshy (eds.), 'The Growth and Transformation of Small Firms in India', Oxford University Press, New Delhi.

Government of India (2005 and 2009), "Handbook of Industrial Policy and Statistics", Ministry of Industry, New Delhi.

Nair, Tara and Keshab Das (2015), "Financing the MSME Sector in India: Approaches, Challenges and Options", Working Paper No. 230, Gujarat Institute of Development Research, Ahmedabad.

Reserve Bank of India (RBI), "Handbook of Statistics on Indian Economy", Mumbai, various issues.

4

Opportunities and Challenges for the Growth of MSMEs in India

Radha Raghuramapatruni

Introduction

Micro, small and medium enterprises (MSME) sector has emerged as a highly vibrant and dynamic sector of the Indian economy. MSMEs not only play a crucial role in providing large employment opportunities at comparatively lower capital cost than large industries, but also help in industrialization of rural and backward areas, thereby, reducing regional imbalances, assuring more equitable distribution of national income and wealth. The MSME sector in India is highly heterogeneous in terms of size of the enterprises, variety of products and services, and levels of technology. MSMEs are complementary to large industries as ancillary units and this sector contributes enormously to the socio-economic development of the country.

The MSME sector is an important pillar of the Indian economy as it contributes greatly to the growth of Indian economy with a vast network of around 30 million units, creating employment of about 70 million, manufacturing more than 8,000 products, contributing about 45 percent to manufacturing output and about 43 percent of exports, directly and indirectly. SME sector contributes to around 15 to 16 percent of India's GDP and is expected to touch a figure of 22 percent in the next 3 years. Nearly 60 percent of the SMEs in India fall in the unorganized sector, once this untapped potential becomes the source for growth of these, the size of Indian GDP can surpass that of the developed nations.

This sector even assumes greater importance now as the country moves towards a faster and inclusive growth agenda. Moreover, it is the MSME sector which can help realize the target of proposed National Manufacturing Policy of raising the share of manufacturing sector in GDP from 16 percent at present to 25 percent by the end of 2022. The present paper is an attempt to focus on the current status of performance of MSMEs in India and highlights the major challenges for the growth of MSMEs and initiatives taken to solve constraints both at the government and the institutional level.

Review of Literature

Amit Shanbaug (2015) observed that the small and medium enterprises (SMEs) play a vital role in the growth of Indian economy by contributing to about 45 percent of the industrial output, 40 percent of exports, 42 million in employment, creating one million jobs every year and producing more than 8,000 quality products for the Indian and international markets.

Sanjay Kumar Dey (2014) observed that the small and medium enterprises (SMEs) contribute to economic development in various ways such as creating employment opportunities for the rural and urban population, providing goods and services at affordable costs by offering innovative solutions and sustainable development to the economy. However, he viewed that the sector faces a number of problems which include absence of adequate and timely banking finance, non-availability of suitable technology, ineffective marketing due to limited resources and non-availability of skilled manpower.

Gandhi (2014) in his key note speech *Structure of Foreign Banks for Emerging Nations: The Indian Case* at the ASIFMA Annual Conference in November 2014, emphasized the need for a positive support from foreign banks for lending to export and the SSI sector in India.

Venkatesh and Muthiah (2012) found that the role of small

and medium enterprises (SMEs) in the industrial sector is growing rapidly and that they have become a thrust area for future growth. They emphasized that nurturing the SME sector is essential for the economic well-being of the nation. The above literature highlights various aspects viz. performance, growth and problems of MSMEs in the Indian economy and induces for continuous research in this field.

Singh et al. (2012) analyzed the performance of small-scale industry in India and focused on policy changes which have opened up new opportunities for this sector. Their study concluded that SSI sector has made good progress in terms of the number of SSI units, production and employment levels. The study recommended the emergence of technology development and strengthening of financial infrastructure to boost SSI sector and achieve the desired growth target.

Dixit and Pandey (2011) applied co-integration analysis to examine the causal relationship between SMEs output, exports, employment, number of SMEs and their fixed investment and India's GDP, total exports and employment (public and private) for the period 1973-74 to 2006-07. Their study revealed a positive causality between SMEs output and India's GDP.

Bargal et al. (2009) examined the causal relationship among the three variables GDP, SSI output and SSI exports and also compared the performance parameters of SSIs in the pre- and post-liberalization era. The study found that the annual average growth rate of different parameters of SSIs have declined in the period of nineties vis-à-vis the pre-reform years. There is an absence of any lead-lag causal relationship between exports and production in small-scale sector and GDP of the Indian economy.

Thorsten Beck (2008) finds that institutions find the SME segment to be highly profitable, but perceived macroeconomic instability in developing countries and competition in developed countries as the main obstacles.

Objectives of the Study

1. To analyse the growth of employment, output, promotion of exports of MSMEs in India.
2. To study the key challenges faced by the MSMEs sector.
3. To assess the performance of MSMEs in India and prospects for future growth.

The present research study is "exploratory" in nature. The study is primarily based on the secondary data covering 8 years from 2007-08 to 2014-15. All the financial data are compiled from annual reports of the Ministry of MSMEs, Government of India, different books and periodicals. Further, the articles and information available in different journals and magazines were also referred to.

Definitions

Small -scale Industrial Unit: An industrial undertaking, in which the investment is fixed assets in plant and machinery, whether held on ownership terms, or on lease, or by hire-purchase, does not exceed ₹ 100 lakh as on March 31, 2001, is to be treated as a small-scale industrial unit.

Micro, Small and Medium Enterprises (MSMEs): MSME sector consists of any enterprises, whether proprietorship, Hindu undivided family, association of persons, co-operative society, partnership or undertaking or any other legal entity, by whatever name called, engaged in production of goods pertaining to any industry specified in the first schedule of Industries Development and Regulation Act, 1951 and other enterprises engaged in production and rendering of services. Under the Micro, Small and Medium Enterprises Development Act, 2006, MSMEs are classified as shown in Table 4.1.

Major Players: In spite of their limitations, the SMEs have made a significant contribution towards technological development and exports. They are present in almost all major sectors of the Indian industry such as, food processing, textiles and garments, agricultural inputs, leather and leather goods, chemicals and pharmaceuticals, bio-engineering, engineering, electricals, sports goods, electronics, plastics products, electro-medical equipment, computer software etc.

Table 4.1: Classification of MSMEs

Enterprises	Investment in Plant and Machinery (Manufacturing)	Investment in Equipment (Services)
Micro	Up to ₹ 25 lakh	Up to ₹ 10 lakh
Small	Above ₹ 25 lakh and up to ₹ 5 crore	Above ₹ 10 lakh and up to ₹ 2 crore
Medium	Above ₹ 5 crore and up to ₹ 10 crore	Above ₹ 2 crore and up to ₹ 5 crore

Evaluation of the Performance of MSME s

As per the provisions of the Act, all MSMEs are required to file an entrepreneurs memorandum (Part-I) at the District Industries Centres (DICs). After commencement of the project, the entrepreneur concerned is required to file an entrepreneurs memorandum (Part-II) [EM (Part-II)]. Prior to enactment of the MSMED Act, 2006, there was a system of registration of small-scale industrial units by the DICs. Sector-wise i.e., micro, small, and medium details of EM-II filed with the Commissionerates/Directorates of Industries during 2007-08 to 2014-15 are given in Table 4.2.

The performance of micro, small and medium enterprises (MSMEs) sector is assessed by the conduct of periodic All-India Census of the Sector. The latest census conducted was the Fourth All-India Census of MSMEs.

The Census was conducted with reference year as 2006-07, wherein the data was collected during the period of 2012-13 and results were published in 2014-15. The scope and coverage of the MSME sector was broadened significantly under the MSMED Act, 2006, which recognized the concept of "enterprise" including both manufacturing and services, besides defining the term medium enterprises under the MSME sector.

Contribution of the MSME sector towards GDP and output is shown in Table 4.3.

Table 4.2: Status of Filing of Entrepreneurs Memorandum (Part II)

Year	Micro	Small	Medium	Total
2007-08	1,53,110	16,730	467	1,72,703
2008-09	1,70,262	18,792	702	1,93,026
2009-10	1,85,180	23,870	1,409	2,13,206
2010-11	2,05,112	29,125	1,263	2,38,429
2011-12	2,42,539	34,225	2,949	2,82,428
2012-13	2,75,867	41,502	5,449	3,22818
2013-14	2,96,526	59,127	7,338	3,62,991
2014-15	3,46,206	70,933	8,219	4,25,358
Average	2,34,350	36,788	3474.5	2,76,370
CAGR	12 percent	23 percent	51 percent	14 percent

Source: Author's calculations based on the State/UT Commissionerates/Directorates of Industries and MSME-Development Institutes.

Table 4.3: Contribution of the MSME Sector in GDP and Output

Year	Gross Value of Output of MSMEs in the Manufacturing Sector (₹ crore)	Share of the MSMEs Sector in Total GDP (percent)			Share of MSMEs Manufacturing Output in Total Manufacturing Output (percent)
		Manufacturing Sector MSMEs	Services Sector MSMEs	Total	
2006-07	11,98,818	7.73	27.40	35.13	42.02
2007-08	13,22,777	7.81	27.60	35.41	41.98
2008-09	13,75,589	7.52	28.60	36.12	40.79
2009-10	14,88,352	7.45	28.60	36.05	39.63
2010-11	16,53,622	7.39	29.30	36.69	38.50
2011-12	17,88,584	7.27	30.70	37.97	37.47
2012-13	18,09,976	7.04	30.50	37.54	37.33

Source: The State/UT Commissionerates/Directorates of Industries and MSME-Development Institutes.

It is discernible from Table 4.4 that the number of enterprises, employment, investment in fixed assets and gross output of MSME units in India show an increasing trend over the nine year period. From the financial year 2006-07, figures include activities of wholesale/retail trade, legal, education and social services, hotels and restaurants, transport and storage and warehousing (except cold storage) for which data was extracted from the Economic Census, 2005, Central Statistics Office (CSO), Ministry of Statistics and Programme Implementation, Government of India. Number of enterprises and employment registered an annual growth of approximately 14 percent whereas the value of fixed assets and output witnessed a growth of approximately 7 percent.

Table 4.4: Performance of SSIs/MSMEs Employment and Investments

S. No.	Year	Total Working Enterprises (in lakhs)	Employment (in lakhs)	Market Value of Fixed Assets (₹ crore)
1.	2006-07	361.76	805.23	868,543.79
2.	2007-08	377.36	842.00	920,459.84
3.	2008-09	393.70	880.84	977,114.72
4.	2009-10	410.80	921.79	1,038,546.08
5.	2010-11	428.73	965.15	1,105,934.09
6.	2011-12	447.64	1,011.69	1,182,757.64
7.	2012-13	467.54	1,061.40	1,268,763.67
8.	2013-14	488.46	1,114.29	1,363,700.54
9.	2014-15	510.57	1,171.32	1,471,912.94
Average		431.84	974.8567	11,33,081.48
CAGR		4 percent	5 percent	7 percent

Source: Author's calculations based on State/UT Commissionerates or Directorates of Industries and MSME-Development Institutes.

Key Challenges Faced by the MSME Sector

Despite its commendable contribution to the nation's economy, the MSME sector does not get the required support from the concerned Government departments, banks, financial institutions and corporates, which is a handicap in their becoming more competitive at the national and international level. Few important factors hampering their growth include:

- Lack of availability of adequate and timely credit.
- High cost of credit.
- Collateral requirements.

- Limited access to equity capital.
- Procurement of raw material at a competitive cost.
- Problems of storage, designing, and product display.
- Lack of access to global markets.
- Inadequate infrastructure facilities, including power, water, roads, etc.
- Low technology levels and lack of access to modern technology.
- Lack of skilled manpower for manufacturing, services, marketing, etc.
- Multiplicity of labour laws and complicated procedures associated with compliance of such laws.

Despite the various challenges it has been facing, the MSME sector has shown admirable innovativeness, adaptability and resilience to survive the recent economic downturn and recession.

Major Recommendations for the Growth of MSMEs

A suggested framework to help minimise the challenges faced by MSMEs in their growth is outlined below.

- **Introduction of Easy Financing and Credit Tools:** In order to compete with large scale enterprises and other global counterparts, it is important that they are provided easy and affordable funding opportunities to obtain credit. With limited working capital, key for MSMEs is the availability of low cost finance from public sector banks (PSBs). In order to retain growth for the MSMEs, the government must work towards establishing an environment that simplifies access to finance and creates transparency in how banks and credit agencies decide the sanction of credit. The measures taken by the government should be such that it is easy for the MSMEs to obtain a term loan from banks without high emphasis on collaterals and complex paperwork and at reduced interest rates. The measures should include standard project appraisal system in banks, reduced transaction costs in imports/exports, and encouragement for cluster financing by creating MSME hubs and insurance coverage to banks.

- **Developing a Supporting Legal and Regulatory Framework:** An effective legal and regulatory framework promotes competition by avoiding overly restrictive licensing requirements and allows international and regional banks with better MSME lending tools to enter the market. Competition among financial sector players can be promoted further by introducing technological platforms in key areas, facilitating a variety of financial products and services, driving down the costs of financial access, and reaching previously untapped markets. Frequent revision of Companies' Law and the enactment of bankruptcy legislation will have a highly positive impact on MSMEs and the lenders.
- **Access to Modern Affordable Technology:** MSMEs have a unique problem to solve—while they are required to adhere to global standards and ensure compliance to regulations, they mostly have limited understanding (and budgets) for technology. This surely needs to change and Indian MSMEs need to evolve as aggressive users of technology. From being an enabler of productivity and quality, technology must be used for transformation and as a key influencer for competitive advantage. MSMEs expect the Government to take necessary steps to provide modern technology at cheaper and subsidized cost, enable ecosystem to facilitate technology transfer, and create a platform for technology providers and technology seekers. The Government needs to create and collate public information and systems towards technological base.
- **Strengthening the Financial Infrastructure:** Establishing a solid financial infrastructure (auditing and accounting standards, credit registries/bureaus, collateral, and insolvency regimes) should be a priority in financial development. The aim should be to develop a comprehensive credit reporting system that covers both personal and commercial credit

information, and help lenders better manage credit risk and extend access to credit. Some countries, such as India, have introduced MSME rating agencies as an additional institution designed to provide more information to prospective lenders. Moreover, a well-functioning collateral regime characterized by a wide range of allowable collaterals (immovable and movables), the establishment of clear priority rankings of claims over collateral, efficient collateral registries making priority interests publicly known, and effective enforcement of collateral in the case of default can further enhance risk acceptability of MSME customers by financial institutions. Institutions for financers' specific training in small credit and MSMEs financing requirement should be set up by every PSB.

- **Effective Government Support Mechanism**s: In all cases, government interventions should be carefully designed and better evaluated with a view to accurately measure their achievements in terms of outreach and leverage. Partial credit guarantee schemes should remain an important form of intervention. Key guiding principles on such schemes should contain guidelines on eligibility criteria, coverage ratios, scalable credit approval mechanism, fees, payment rules, use of collateral/down payment, and equity ratios, among other parameters.
- **Access to Marketing Platforms and Networks:** The need for enterprises to increase market coverage, improve operational efficiencies and enhance customer engagement is imperative. However, this requires readiness on two accounts—the company and government regulations and policies including SME special programs, initiatives and funds.
- **Introducing Labour Law Reforms:** The last few years have seen an exponential growth in the inflow of workers into the MSME sector; this speaks volumes about the potential that MSMEs hold for national development. The presence of flexible labour laws therefore becomes

increasingly critical in today's environment. Labour law provisions such as standardized wages, social security, and job safety ensure that the workforce is protected and delivers its highest output. MSMEs require government-led initiatives and schemes for competency and skill development to ensure that they do not have under-skilled workers.

Conclusion

Small and medium enterprises (SMEs) contribute to the economic development in various ways such as creating employment opportunities for rural and urban population, providing goods and services at affordable costs by offering innovative solutions and sustainable development to the economy by contributing around 15 to 16 percent towards the Indian GDP; this figure is expected to reach 22 percent in the next three years.

The sector accounts for about 45 percent of the manufacturing output and 43 percent of total exports of the country. The definition and coverage of the MSME sector was broadened by the MSME Development Act, 2006, which recognized the concept of the an 'enterprise' to include both manufacturing and the services sector, besides defining medium enterprises and setting up a Board for developing policy frameworks and indicating procurement policy.

However, as a whole, MSMEs in India face a number of problems such as absence of adequate and timely bank finance, non-availability of suitable technology, ineffective marketing due to limited resources and non-availability of skilled manpower. To make this sector become more vibrant and a significant player in the development of the Indian economy, the Government of India has taken various initiatives. The recent *Make in India* campaign too focuses on several skill enhancement initiatives and supports the MSME sector. However, a lot is expected and much needs to be done for the growth and development of the MSMEs in India.

References

Bala Subrahmanya, M.H. (2004), "Small Industry and Globalization: Implications, Performance and Prospects", *Economic and Political Weekly*, Volume XXXIX, No.18, pp. 1826-1834.

Bargal, H., Dashmishra, M., and Sharma, A. (2009), "Performance Analysis of Small Scale Industries: A Study of Pre-liberalization and Post-liberalization Period", *International Journal of Business and Management*, Volume 1, No. 2.

Dixit, A. and Pandey, A.K. (2011), "SMEs and Economic Growth in India: Co-integration Analysis", *The IUP Journal of Financial Economics*, Volume IX, No. 2, pp. 41-59.

Gandhi, R. (2014) "Structure of Foreign Banks for Emerging Nations-Indian Case", ASIFMA Annual Conference, November.

Singh, R., Verma, O.P. and Anjum, B. (2012), "Small Scale Industry: An Engine of Growth", *Zenith International Journal of Business Economics and Management Research*, Volume 2, Issue 5, available at:
http://www.zenithresearch.org.in.

Venkatesh, S. and Muthiah, K. (2012), "SMEs in India: Importance and Contribution", *Asian Journal of Management Research*, Volume 2, No. 2.

Lubina Zaidi (2013), "Problems Affecting the Growth of Small and Medium Enterprises (SMEs) in India", International Conference on Technology and Business Management, March 18-20, pp. 413-422.

Mali, D.D. (1998), "Development of Micro, Small and Medium Enterprises of India: Current Scenario and Challenges", *SEDME (Small Enterprises Development, Management and Extension) Journal*, Volume 25, No. 4.

"The SME Whitebook 2011-2012", *Business World*, New Delhi.

Raju, B. Yerram and Nataraj, P.R. Mohan (2008), "Small and Medium Enterprises in India", Indian Institute of Banking and Finance.

Sanjeeb Kumar Dey (2014), "MSMEs in India: Its Growth and Prospects", *Abhinav National Monthly Refereed Journal of Research in Commerce and Management*, Volume 3, Issue. 8, August.

Amit Shanbaug (2015), "Growth Drivers for TOM", *The Times of India*, March 8.

"Small and Medium Business Development Chamber of India",

available at:
http://www.smechamberofindia.com/About_MSMEs.aspx.

"Annual Report on MSMEs, 2011-12, 2012-13, 2013-14 and 2014-15", Government of India, New Delhi.

"Report of the Working Group on MSMEs Growth in Twelfth Five Year Plan: 2012-17", Government of India, New Delhi.

5

Dynamic Nexus between MSME Sector and Economic Growth in India

S.K. Mishra and P.K. Mishra

Introduction

Since a long time, it has been observed by planners, policymakers, academicians, and researchers that small and medium enterprises (SMEs)/micro, small and medium enterprises (MSMEs) play a significant role in the economic development of underdeveloped as well as developed economies. MSMEs are helpful in building the superstructure of the industrial sector in an economy (Katua, 2014). Feeney and Riding (1997) noted that small and medium enterprises play an important role in the development of a country. Both developed and underdeveloped nations emphasize on the critical role that they play in the sustainable economic development process for their utilization of indigenous resources, substantial contributions to domestic production, low investment requirements, creating ample employment opportunities, contributions to infrastructure building and regional development, and significant export earnings (Bhati, 2002; Muritala et al., 2012; Tirkey, 2012; Uma, 2013; Rajan, 2013; Lakshmi, 2013; Susmitha, 2014; Katua, 2014).

Thus, SMEs/MSMEs are crucial in economic development of a country. These are the means by which productive activities that are indigenously owned and controlled, and also the productive resources and talents are used (Agbonifor, 1998).

SMEs/MSMEs are often interpreted as the solution for economic progress, modernization and the growth of employment, creation of income, and development of science and technology in most advanced economies (Neck and Dockner, 1987; Acs and Audretsch, 1990; Kotey and Meredith, 1997, Bhutta and Asad, 2008). Fida (2008) observed that SMEs contribute to economic development in various ways: by creating employment for rural and urban labour force, providing desirable sustainability, and innovation in the economy as a whole.

It is generally agreed that the development of micro and small-scale enterprises can be a key ingredient in poverty-reduction (Sen, 1980; Green et al., 2002). Empirical evidence shows that small-scale enterprises contribute significantly to household incomes (Lied et al., 1994; McPherson, 1996; Kapoor et al., 1997; Perks, 2004; McDade and Spring, 2005). UNCTAD (2001) affirms that countries with a high rate of small industrial enterprises have succeeded in making the income distribution (both regionally and functionally) more equitable. The small-scale industries, due to their widespread existence and large employment potential, ensure equitable distribution of income and wealth in an economy (Lakshmi, 2013).

It is evident globally that a well-organized SME sector is favourable to rapid industrial intensification (Hill, 2001; Llyod, 2002). MSMEs serve as a useful bridgehead between the informal economy of family enterprise and the formalised corporate sector. They support the growth of large industries by providing them components, accessories and semi-finished goods.

According to Beck et al. (2005), SMEs enhance competition and entrepreneurship. Thus, they have external benefits on economy wide efficiency, innovation and aggregate productivity. They are the primary vehicles by which new entrepreneurs provide the economy with a continuous supply of ideas, skills, and innovations (CACCI, 2003). Empirical studies show that new firms play a significant role in employment generation (e.g. Garikai, 2011; Baptista et al., 2005; Stel and Suddle, 2005), innovation (e.g. Fritsch and Mueller, 2005), economic growth and reduction of unemployment (e.g. Garikai, 2011).

According to Muragia (2008), entrepreneurs in America are respected for their role in creating new jobs, providing competition to existing businesses, improving product quality, reducing prices, and introducing new goods and services through innovation and technology advancement. Thus, the significance of SMEs in the world economy cannot be underestimated because they are the most important sources to reduce poverty, improve growth in the national economy, provide basic source of employment and enhance upward social mobility (Akhtar et al., 2011).

The role of SMEs is significant in many countries. Economic growth in developed and developing countries such as Japan, Korea, Taiwan and many others, was significantly generated by SME activities. The percentage contribution of SMEs to gross domestic product/total value added ranges from 60 percent in China, 57 percent in Germany, 55.3 percent in Japan and 50 percent in Korea, compared to 47.3 percent attained by Malaysia. SMEs have also played a very important role in the economic development of China. At present, there are more than 10 million SMEs comprising, 99 percent of the total number of enterprises in China. SMEs contribute 60 percent of industrial output volume and 40 percent of the total taxes and profits realized by enterprises in China.

The contribution of SMEs in output of Japan is 65 percent, Germany 48 percent while in the US, it is 45 percent. SMEs in the US generate more than half of the nation's gross domestic product (Katua, 2014). In Netherlands, SMEs account for 98.8 percent of all private sector companies, contribute 31.6 percent to gross domestic product, and employ 55 percent of total workforce (EIM Business and Policy Research, 1999; Indarti and Langenberg, 2004). In Australia, small businesses account for approximately 97 percent of all private sector businesses, and 51 percent of private sector employment (Australian Bureau of Statistics, 1996; Wijewardena and Tibbits, 1999). In Italy, SMEs contribute US$ 35 million in exports and absorb 2.2 million of national labour force (Patrianila, 2003; Indarti and Langenberg, 2004). Evidence shows that SMEs contribute to 32 percent of gross domestic product, 56.4 percent to employment opportunities and 19 percent to exports in Malaysia (SMIDEC, 2008; Omar et al., 2009).

According to the Indonesian statistics, in 2003, the number of Indonesian SMEs was 42.4 million and they contributed 56.7 percent to GDP, accounting for 19.4 percent of total exports, and employing 79 million of work force (BPS and KUKM, 2003; Indarti and Langenberg, 2004). As indicated by the Small and Medium Enterprises Development Authority (SMEDA), the SME sector of Pakistan represents approximately 90 percent of all the enterprises in Pakistan. SMEs almost employed 80 percent of the non-agricultural work force, and shared about 40 percent in the annual GDP of the country (Malik et al., 2011).

It is, therefore, discerned that micro, small and medium enterprises play a crucial role in the process of industrialization and economic growth and development of both developing and the developed nations. These industries by and large represent a stage in economic transition from traditional segments to modern segments. The MSMEs play a vital role for the growth of Indian economy by contributing 45 percent of the industrial output, 40 percent of exports, providing employment to 42 million people, and creating one million jobs every year and a range of more than 8,000 quality products for the Indian and international markets (Singh et al., 2015).

Looking at the veritable importance of small businesses, MSMEs can be considered as catalysts for economic development of an emerging market economy like India. It is in this backdrop, the paper is an attempt to make an empirical investigation of the dynamic nexus between the performance of MSMEs in India and real economic development of the country.

Performance of MSMEs in India: An Overview

Since a long time, small-scale industries have been given a credible place in economics science for the important roles that they play by creating ample employment opportunities, contributing to GDP, promoting exports and alleviating poverty while industrialising the nation. SSIs/MSMEs are basically labour-intensive and adaptable to local conditions (Garg, 1996). Consequently, the Government of India has given SSI/MSME sector an important place while chalking out the various Five Year Plans and enacting the various industrial policy resolutions.

India has been giving special importance to small-scale industries (SSIs) which has recently been replaced by the MSMEs with the enactment of Micro, Small and Medium Enterprises Development Act, 2006. The GoI has recognised MSMEs critical contribution in providing large scale employment opportunities at comparatively lower capital cost than large industries, industrialization of rural and backward areas thereby reducing regional imbalances, and assuring more equitable distribution of national income and wealth (GoI, 2016). MSMEs have been considered complementary to large industries as ancillary units, and a contributor to the socio-economic development of the country (GoI, 2016).

The onset of the planning era in 1951 saw the village and small-scale industries sector being recognised as an important tool for employment generation and balanced regional development (Hameed, 2003). During the Second Five Year Plan (1956-61), as many as 60 small-scale industrial houses were established, and certain items were reserved for exclusive manufacture in small-scale sector. During the Third Five Year Plan (1961-66), the SSI Board constituted a working group to formulate a plan for the development of small-scale industries.

The Fourth Five Year Plan (1969-74) document states that the main aim of the development programmes for small-scale industries was fuller utilization of the capacity already established, intensive development of selected industries including ancillaries and industrial co-operatives and subject to criteria of feasibility, promotion of industries in semi-urban, rural and backward areas.

The Fifth Five Year Plan (1974-79) stressed the development of different small industries so as to remove poverty, generate employment and reduce inequalities. The Sixth Five Year Plan (1980-85) emphasized the shift from industrial development through publicly owned large industrial units to assist for expansion of small-scale private industrial units so as to improve the levels of productions and earnings. The Seventh Five Year Plan (1985-90) laid stress on technology upgradation, and comprehensive marketing support to small-scale industries.

The Eighth Five Year Plan (1992-97) stressed on timely and adequate availability of credit, and infrastructure development for the growth of SSIs in a liberalised, privatised and globalised framework. And, Ninth Plan onwards, the Government of India has constructively emphasized on the strength to strength growth of small-scale industries through several reforms, policies, and programmes.

The industrial sector of the Indian economy has undergone a paradigm shift with the enactment of Micro, Small and Medium Enterprises Development Act, 2006. The objective was to promote and improve competitiveness of SMEs in the country. The MSMEs in India, which constitute more than 90 percent of the total number of industrial enterprises, form the backbone of industrial development.

It has emerged as a highly vibrant and dynamic sector of the Indian economy which contributes nearly 38 percent of the country's overall GDP, 45 percent of the manufacturing output and 40 percent of the exports. They provide the largest share of employment after agriculture (Katyal and Xaviour, 2015). The sector provides employment opportunities for around 120 million people, mostly concentrated in rural areas. The MSME sector has the potential to spread industrial growth across the country and can be a major partner in the process of inclusive growth (GoI, 2016).

It is, thus, clear that the growth of SSIs/MSMEs in India is one of the most significant features of the planned economic development of the country. There has been a phenomenal growth of this sector during the last 45 years since 1971-72. It is in this backdrop, that we now proceed to examine the trend pattern of the growth of SMEs/MSMEs (including manufacturing and services) in Indian economy during 1971-72 to 2013-14 dividing the entire period into three sub-periods, viz., 1971-72 to 1989-90 (pre-liberalization period), 1991-92 to 2005-06 (liberalization period), and 2006-07 to 2013-14 (post-MSME Development Act period).

Establishment of SSI/MSME Units

The data clearly exhibits a rising trend of establishment of SSI/MSME units in India over the period from 1971-72 to 2013-14 with upward leaps in the liberalization period, and with larger leaps after the enactment of MSME Development Act, 2006 (Figure 5.1). However, the annual growth rate is almost stationary during each sub-period. This calls for more focus of policymakers on the expansion of the MSME sector in India.

Trend Pattern of MSME Production: The production of output by the SSI/MSME sector in India has shown an upward surge during 1971-72 to 2013-14 with a rising trend during the pre-liberalization period, a temporary slowdown in the first half of 1990s, a good spurt since the second half of 1990s, and an upward moving trend after the enactment of MSME Development Act, 2006 (Figure 5.2).

Trend Pattern of MSME Employment and Productivity: In India, the manpower employment contribution of SSI/MSME sector to total employment in the country is very significant. A sustained upward trend of employment in the SSI/MSME sector is observed during 1971-72 and 2013-14 with little deviations in short-periods (Figure 5.3). Certainly, implementation of economic reforms in early 1990s has contributed to a rising trend in manpower employment in MSME sector in India. And, this has shown further hikes with an upward jerk after the enactment of MSME Development Act, 2006.

Figure 5.1: Trend Pattern of SSI/MSME Units in India

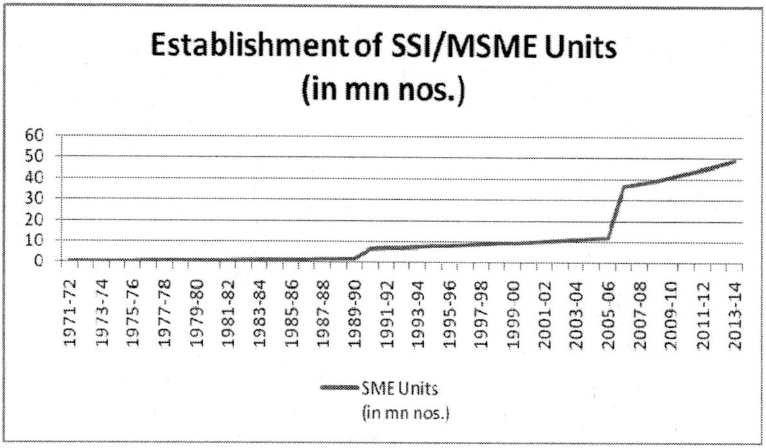

Source: Authors' own plot.

Figure 5.2: Trend Pattern of Production in MSME Sector in India

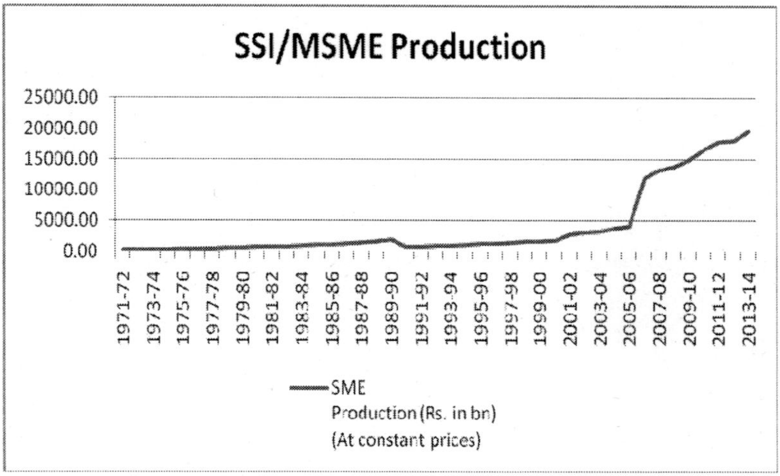

Source: Authors' own plot.

Figure 5.3: Trend Pattern of Employment in MSME Sector in India

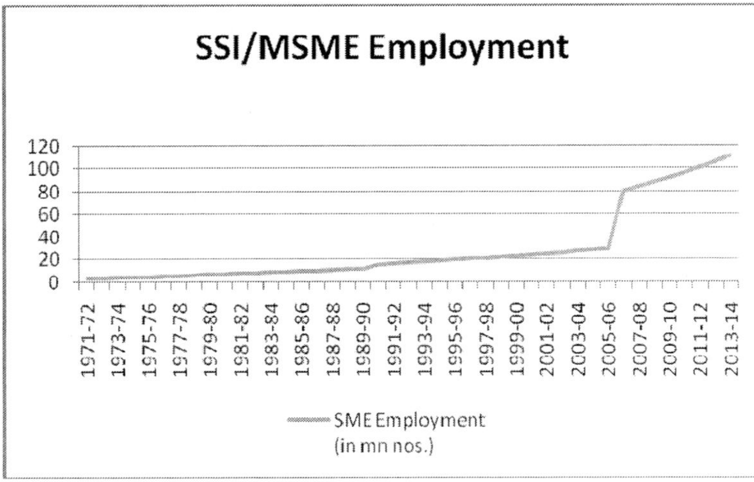

Source: Authors' own plot.

The productivity per worker in this sector also shows similar pattern of growth over the sample period of study (Figure 5.4). This clearly indicates the development of skill, influence of technological progress, benefits of division of labour and specialization, favourable working environment, positive effects of government rules and regulations concerning the development of MSME sector in India.

Trend Pattern of MSME Fixed Investment: The SSI/MSME sector in India has shown a rising trend in fixed investments over the period 1971-72 to 2013-14 with a sluggish growth rate during the pre-liberalization era, and a slowly rising growth trend in the liberalization period (Figure 5.5). But after the enactment of the MSME Development Act, 2006, data exhibits an upward surge in fixed investment in the MSME sector in India.

Now, it is essential to see whether such growth pattern of fixed investment in SME sector has got any effect on the output of this sector. So, we calculated the production per fixed investment (proxy for capital productivity) and plotted in Figure 5.6. The growth pattern of capital productivity or productivity of fixed investment is quite discouraging throughout the sample period, and more shocking in the post-reform periods.

Figure 5.4: Trend Pattern of Labour Productivity in MSME Sector in India

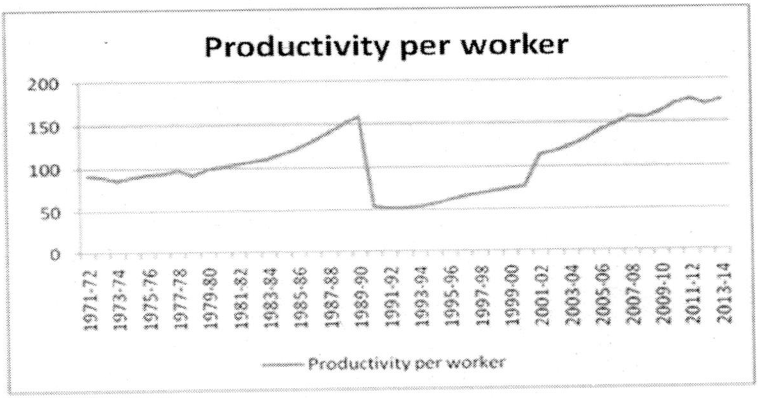

Source: Authors' own plot.

Figure 5.5: Trend Pattern of Fixed Investment in MSME Sector in India

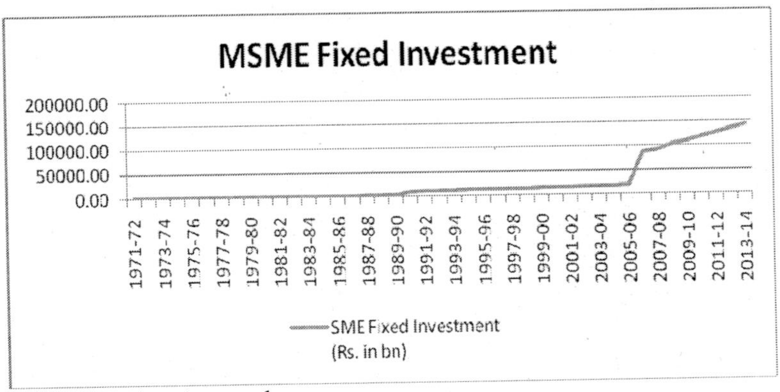

Source: Authors' own plot.

Figure 5.6: Trend Pattern of Capital Productivity in MSME Sector in India

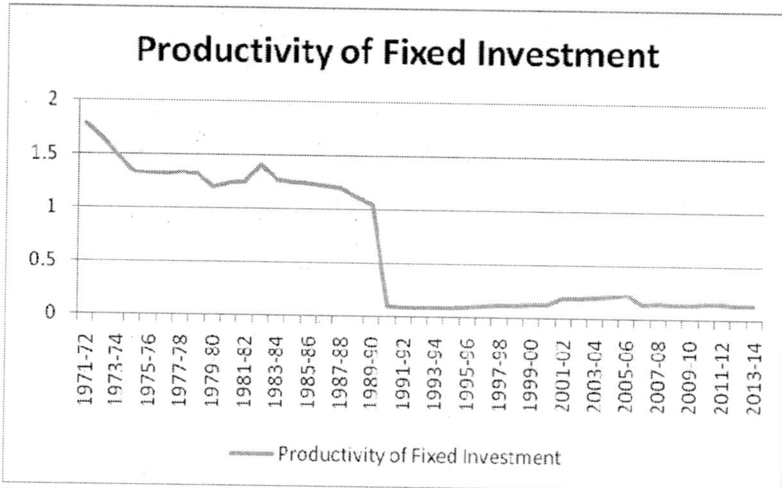

Source: Authors' own plot.

One aspect is that the MSME sector in India is focusing on the capital-saving technology which basically relies on indigenous raw materials and domestic technology which is mostly labour dependent and positively caters to the problems of unemployment. On the contrary, low rate of capital productivity is related to low quality of output, high cost of production, low profitability, and slow growth of the sector. Thus, our objective here is to draw the attention of entrepreneurs, planners and policymakers concerning the low and stagnant growth rate of productivity of fixed investment in the SSI/MSME sector in India.

Trend Pattern of Exports by MSME Sector: In India, the contribution of MSME sector to export basket is quite satisfactory over the years (Figure 5.7). There has been a six fold increase in the growth of exports from the SSI/MSME sector from ₹ 1, 600 crore in 1980-81 to ₹ 9,664 crore in 1990-91. Although, the annual growth rate fluctuated from year to year during the 1980s, the decade of 1990s indicates high growth of exports from the SSI/MSME sector. Exports rose from ₹ 13,883 crore in 1991-92 to ₹ 54,200 crore in 1999-2000 which is almost a four-fold increase during the period. Such an increasing trend continued and made a further take off after the enactment of the MSME Development Act, 2006. Thus, owing to the specific role they are playing in the socio-economic development of the country, MSMEs can be considered home grown MNCs with global footprints (Rajput et al., 2012). They encompass a heterogeneous group of activities in the manufacturing, services, and trade and agri-business sectors. Thus, they can be credited for inclusive and sustainable economic development of India (Rajput et al., 2012).

Figure 5.7: Trend Pattern of Exports in MSME Sector in India

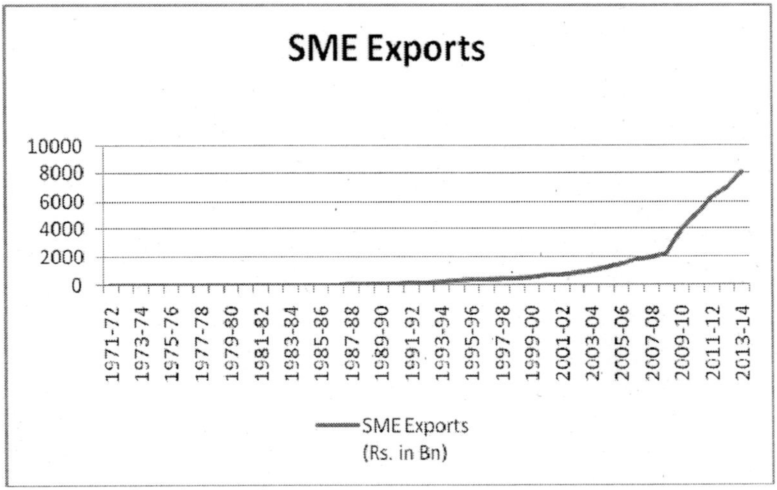

Source: Authors' own plot.

The MSMEs contribute to employment generation, poverty reduction, and equitable growth and development of the national economy. As seen above, the exports from MSME sector have been clocking excellent growth rates in this decade mainly fuelled by performance of garments, leather, gems and jewellery for this sector. The product groups in which MSME sector dominates in the area of exports are sports goods, readymade garments, woollen garments, knitwear, plastic products, processed foods and leather products. Therefore, the MSMEs have been widely accepted as the engines of economic growth, particularly in lesser developed economies.

Data and Methodology

In view of the above mentioned importance of MSMEs in the economic growth and development of an emerging market economy like India, we now turn to examine the co-integrating relationship between MSMEs output, exports, employment, number of MSMEs and their fixed investment and India's real GDP over the sample period spanning from 1982-83 to 2013-14. This sample period includes the pre-liberalization, liberalization and post-MSME Development Act periods. The annual data on gross domestic product at factor cost (GDP), number of units of MSMEs (EST), total MSME production (MQ), employment created by MSMEs (EMP), total exports by MSMEs (EXT) and fixed investments in the MSME sector (INV) in India have been compiled from Handbook of Statistics on Indian Economy published by the RBI, and Handbook of Industrial Statistics and the MSME annual reports published by the GoI. All the variables have been expressed in their natural logarithms to avoid the likely problems of heteroscedasticity (Gujarati, 2007). Thus, the nomenclatures used for the variables in the study are: LGDP, LEST, LINV, LMQ, LEMP, and LEXT.

It is hypothesized that the MSMEs accelerate the economic growth of India through their contributions in terms of establishment of industrial set ups, outputs produced, employment generated, investments absorbed, and exports made. Presuming the existence of a long-run positive relationship between the contributions of MSMEs to real economic growth of India, we suggest the following model to be empirically estimated:

$$LGDP_t = \beta_0 + \beta_1 LEST_t + \beta_2 LINV_t + \beta_3 LEMP_t + \beta_4 LMQ_t + \beta_5 LEXT_t + \varepsilon_t \quad (1)$$

In a time series analysis, it is necessary to test whether the relevant variables in equation (1) are stationary or not. For this purpose, we have used Augmented Dickey-Fuller (ADF) unit root test (Dickey and Fuller 1979, 1981). It consists of running a regression of the first difference of the series against the series lagged once, lagged difference terms and optionally, a constant and a time trend. This can be expressed as:

$$\Delta Y_t = \alpha_0 + \alpha_1 t + \alpha_2 Y_{t-1} + \sum_{j=1}^{p} \alpha_j \Delta Y_{t-j} + \varepsilon_t \quad (2)$$

The additional lagged terms are included to ensure that the errors are uncorrelated. In this ADF procedure, the test for a unit root is conducted on the coefficient of Y_{t-1} in the regression. If the coefficient is significantly different from zero, then the hypothesis that Y_t contains a unit root is rejected. Rejection of the null hypothesis implies stationarity. Precisely, the null hypothesis is that the variable Y_t is a non-stationary series ($H_0 : \alpha_2 = 0$) and is rejected when α_2 is significantly negative ($H_a : \alpha_2 < 0$). If the calculated value of ADF statistic is higher than McKinnon's critical values, then the null hypothesis (H_0) is not rejected and the series is non-stationary or not integrated of order zero, I (0). Alternatively, rejection of the null hypothesis implies stationarity. Failure to reject the null hypothesis leads to conducting the test on the difference of the series, so further differencing is conducted until stationarity is reached and the null hypothesis is rejected. If the time series (variables) are non-stationary in their levels, they can be integrated with I (1), when their first differences are stationary.

In the case when the variables are found non-stationary, equation (1) cannot be estimated by Ordinary Least Squares

(OLS) method, as such estimation may give rise to spurious regression. However, if the variables are co-integrated, then the regression can be estimated by the Dynamic Ordinary Least Squares (DOLS) method as developed by Stock and Watson (1993).

Thus, we have examined the existence co-integration relationship between the variables of interest by using Johansen's co-integration test (Johansen 1988, 1989, 1991, 1995; Johansen and Jusellius 1990). In the Johansen framework, the first step is the estimation of an unrestricted, closed p^{th} order Vector Auto-Regression (VAR) in k variables. The VAR model as considered in this study is:

$$Y_t = A_1 Y_{t-1} + A_2 Y_{t-2} + \ldots.. + A_p Y_{t-p} + BX_t + \varepsilon_t \quad (3)$$

where Y_t is a k-vector of non-stationary I(1) endogenous variables, X_t is a d-vector of exogenous deterministic variables, $A_1 \ldots\ldots\ldots A_p$ *and* B are matrices of coefficients to be estimated, and ε_t is a vector of innovations that may be contemporaneously correlated but are uncorrelated with their own lagged values and uncorrelated with all of the right-hand side variables. Since most of the economic time series are non-stationary in nature, the above stated VAR model is commonly estimated in its first-difference form as:

$$\Delta Y_t = \Pi Y_{t-1} + \sum_{i=1}^{p-1} \Gamma_i \Delta Y_{t-i} + BX_t + \varepsilon_t \quad (4)$$

Where $\Pi = \sum_{i=1}^{p} A_i - I$ & $\Gamma_i = -\sum_{j=i+1}^{p} A_j$. Granger's representation theorem asserts that if the coefficient matrix Π has reduced rank of $r < k$, then there exists $k \times r$ matrices α *and* β each with rank r such that $\Pi = \alpha\beta'$ *and* $\beta' Y_t$ is I (0). r is the number of co-integrating relations (the *co-integrating rank*) and each column of β is the co-integrating

vector. α is the matrix of error correction parameters that measure the speed of adjustments in ΔY_t. The Johansen approach to co-integration test is based on two test statistics:
(a) *Trace Test Statistic*: The trace test statistic can be specified as: $\tau_{trace} = -T \sum_{i=r+1}^{k} \log(1-\lambda_i)$, where λ_i is the ith largest eigenvalue of matrix Π and T is the number of observations. In the trace test, the null hypothesis is that the number of distinct co-integrating vector(s) is less than or equal to the number of co-integration relations (r).
(b) *Maximum Eigenvalue Test:* The maximum eigenvalue test examines the null hypothesis of exactly r co-integrating relations against the alternative of $r+1$ co-integrating relations with the test statistic: $\tau_{\max} = -T \log(1-\lambda_{r+1})$, where λ_{r+1} is the $(r+1)^{th}$ largest squared eigenvalue. In the trace test, the null hypothesis of $r=0$ is tested against the alternative of $r+1$ co-integrating vectors.

Then we estimated the co-integrating regression by DOLS method so as to examine the long-run responsiveness of the dependent variable to changes in the independent variables as specified in equation (1). DOLS method estimates the parameters depicting long-run elasticities with all variables appearing in their logarithmic level forms. DOLS corrects for endogeneity bias using past and future values of the independent variables as additional regressors (Wooldridge, 2000).

At last, we have used the parameter stability test as proposed by Hansen (1992). Specifically, we have used *Lc* test for parameter instability under the null hypothesis of co-integration or stability. This indicates the co-integration or stability of DOLS estimated parameters in the long-run.

Results and Discussion

In line with the methodologies described in the previous

section, we have first tested the stationarity of each time series of our study by ADF unit roots test both at the level form and at first differences with trend and intercept. The results are presented in Table 5.1.

Table 5.1: Results of Augmented Dickey-Fuller Unit Root Test

Variables	Augmented Dickey-Fuller (ADF) Test Statistic			
	Level form with trend and intercept		First difference form with trend and intercept	
LGDP	-2.081	1%: -4.296 5%: -3.568 10%: -3.218	-4.390	1%: -4.296 5%: -3.568 10%: -3.218
LEST	-2.347	1%: -4.284 5%: -3.562 10%: -3.215	-5.613	1%: -4.296 5%: -3.568 10%: -3.218
LINV	-2.141	1%: -4.284 5%: -3.562 10%: -3.215	-5.441	1%: -4.296 5%: -3.568 10%: -3.218
LEMP	-2.017	1%: -4.284 5%: -3.562 10%: -3.215	-5.526	1%: -4.296 5%: -3.568 10%: -3.218
LMQ	-1.413	1%: -4.284 5%: -3.562 10%: -3.215	-5.210	1%: -4.296 5%: -3.568 10%: -3.218
LEXT	-1.514	1%: -4.284 5%: -3.562 10%: -3.215	-4.694	1%: -4.296 5%: -3.568 10%: -3.218

Source: Authors' own estimation.

It is clear that the null hypothesis of no unit roots for the variables cannot be rejected at their level forms; thus, these variables are non-stationary at their level. However, the null hypothesis of no unit roots for all the time series are rejected at their first differences since the ADF test statistic values are less than the critical values at 1 percent level of significances. Thus, the variables in the study are stationary at the first differences, and are integrated of order one, i.e., I (1) (Table 5.2).

Table 5.2: VAR Lag Order Selection Criteria

Lag	LogL	LR	FPE	AIC	SC	HQ
0	56.69279	NA	3.19e-09	-2.534640	-2.281308	-2.443043
1	303.2959	406.8951*	8.72e-14*	-13.06479*	-11.29147*	-12.42362*
2	325.9536	30.58793	1.93e-13	-12.39768	-9.104365	-11.20692
3	359.7164	35.45092	3.06e-13	-12.28582	-7.472513	-10.54548

* indicates lag order selected by the criterion at 5 percent level
Source: Authors' own estimation.

Then, we have resorted to the Johansen's co-integration test. Since this test is very sensitive to lag length, we have estimated the VAR model to determine the optimal lag length. Table 5.3 reports the VAR lag order selection criteria and it indicates that the optimal lag length, based on the sequential modified LR test statistic (LR), Final Prediction Error (FPE), Akaike Information Criterion (AIC), Schwarz Information Criterion (SC) and Hannan-Quinn Information Criterion (HQ) test statistics, is 1 lag. Now, with this optimal lag length, we have estimated the VAR for Johansen's Trace and Maximum Eigen value tests of co-integration, and the results are summarized in Table 5.3.

Table 5.3: Results of Johansen's Co-integration Test

Hypothesized Number of Cointegrating Equations	Eigen Value	Trace Statistics	Critical Value at 5 percent level (p-value)	Maximum Eigen statistics	Critical Value at 5 percent (p-value)
None *	0.794	112.91	95.75(0.002)	47.51	40.07(0.006)
At most 1	0.596	65.39	69.81(0.107)	27.24	33.87(0.250)
At most 2	0.428	38.14	47.85(0.295)	16.77	27.58(0.599)
At most 3	0.337	21.37	29.79(0.335)	12.34	21.13(0.514)
At most 4	0.258	9.02	15.49(0.363)	8.96	14.26(0.289)
At most 5	0.002	0.06	3.84(0.801)	0.06	3.84(0.801)

*Denotes rejection of the hypothesis at the 0.05 level
Source: Authors' own estimation.

As shown in Table 5.3, the Trace and maximum Eigen value tests indicate the existence of 1 co-integrating equation at 5 percent level of significance. Thus, we can say that there exists the long-run equilibrium relationship between the growth of MSME sector and real economic growth of India. Thus, it is logical to examine the long-run impact of the MSME sector on economic growth of India. So, in order to judge the long-run impact of the growth of MSME sector on economic growth in India, we have estimated the co-integrating regression by DOLS method, and the results are reported in Table 5.4.

Table 5.4: Results of Dynamic OLS Estimation

Dependent Variable: LGDP; Method of Estimation: Dynamic OLS				
Variable	**Coefficient**	**Std. Error**	**t-Statistic**	**Prob.**
C	10.07539	0.104093	96.79197	0.0001
LEST	0.478965	0.012863	37.23493	0.0007
LINV	-0.400110	0.014897	-26.85764	0.0014
LEMP	0.196855	0.032029	6.146145	0.0255
LMQ	0.054367	0.014909	3.646587	0.0677
LEXT	0.262522	0.009136	28.73337	0.0012
R-squared	0.999981	**Mean dependent variable**	10.00986	
Adjusted R-squared	0.999738	**S.D. dependent variable**	0.520184	
S.E. of regression	0.008414	**Sum squared residual**	0.000142	
Long-run variance	4.41E-07			

Source: Authors' own estimation.

In this estimation, the I(1) dependent variable representing real economic growth of India is LGDP, and the independent variables together representing MSME sector development in the country are LEST, LINV, LEMP, LMQ and LEXT. It is revealed from the DOLS estimation that there is a significant and positive long-run relationship between the growth of MSME sector and economic growth in India. Precisely, the establishment of MSMEs, jobs created by MSMEs, output produced by MSMEs and the exports by MSMEs in India have power to explain the economic growth of the country. It is inferred from Table 5.4 that 10 percent increase in the number of MSMEs in the country can lead to about 4.78 percent increase in economic growth in the long-run.

Similarly, 10 percent increase in jobs by MSME sector in the country can lead to 1.96 percent increase in economic growth in the long-run. Furthermore, 10 percent increase in output of MSMEs in India can lead to 0.54 percent increase in economic growth in the long-run. Also, 10 percent increase in exports by MSME sector can lead to 2.62 percent increase in economic growth of the country in the long-run. Contrast to all these, it is found that the fixed investments by MSME sector has a negative and statistically significant impact on the real economic growth of India. However, such statistical finding with respect to the fixed investment should not be generalized for policy making.

Overall, the DOLS results provide the evidence in favour of the positive impact of MSME sector on the real economic growth of India in the long-run. Additionally, R-squared value is 0.999 which is close to 1. It means the aforesaid relationships are very strong over the sample period. In order to ensure reliability in the above estimated DOLS model, the diagnostics of the model must be examined. The high value of R^2 indicates that variations in economic growth are fully explained by the indicators of MSME sector in the long-run. In the long-run, it is essential that the variables depict a stable equilibrium relationship.

For this purpose, we have used *Lc* parameter instability test for the null hypothesis of stability or co-integration as proposed by Hansen (1992). The results of this test are presented in Table 5.5.

The *Lc* statistic cannot reject the null hypothesis at the 1 percent critical level based on DOLS. In other words, the results in Table 5.5 show the evidence for parameter stability as the probability values are greater than 0.05. Thus, the estimated long-run relationship by DOLS is stable.

Table 5.5: Results of Hansen's Parameter Instability Test

Time Series: LGDP, LEST, LINV, LEMP, LMQ, LEXT Null Hypothesis: Series are Co-integrated				
Lc Statistic	Stochastic Trends (m)	Deterministic Trends (k)	Excluded Trends (p2)	Prob.*
0.407270	5	0	0	> 0.2
*Hansen (1992) Lc(m2=4, k=0) p-values, where m2=m-p2 is the number of stochastic trends in the asymptotic distribution				

Source: Authors' own estimation.

Concluding Remarks

In the present era of liberalization and globalization, micro, small and medium enterprises provide an important source of domestic employment creation, resilience against external economic fluctuations, and mechanism for local capacity building through promotion of entrepreneurship. Thus, MSMEs have been recognised as the engine of economic growth and for promoting inclusive development, particularly in developing economies like India. The sector is significant for unemployment reduction, poverty alleviation, and ensuring balanced regional development. In India, MSME sector has emerged as a highly vibrant and dynamic sector of the economy over the last few decades.

This motivated us to undertake a study of this kind which by examining the performance of MSME sector in terms of the number of MSME units, fixed investments, employment creations, output and export contributions, investigate the long-run impact of this sector on the real economic growth of Indian economy in a dynamic framework. The results provide the evidence of a positive impact of MSME sector on the long-run economic growth of India. This gives rise to the policy implication that the MSME sector should be strategically promoted and mobilised for achieving long-run inclusive and sustainable development of the country. In this direction, the Government of India has taken several initiatives since 2006-07.

The registration process of new MSME units has been simplified; strategies have been devised for the revival and rehabilitation of sick units; a network of technology centres and incubation centres have been set up for the promotion of innovation and entrepreneurship especially in rural and agriculture dominated areas; policies for providing financial, technical, and marketing supports; and emphasis on skill development, infrastructure development, etc. are important among others. Our study provides an empirical support to all these policy measures of the Government of India for the development of the MSME sector. However, more intensified focus is warranted in this direction, emphasizing the creation of general awareness regarding small entrepreneurship particularly among the youth, provision of specialized training and skill development, provision of basic utility services, provision of affordable credit, sustained marketing support through brand building, and provision of fiscal incentives such as tax relief, subsidies, etc. All these can go a long way in making the MSME sector as an engine of long-run economic growth and development of India.

References

Acs, Z.J. and D.B. Audretsch (1990), "The Determinants of Small-firm Growth in US Manufacturing", *Applied Economics*, 22(2): 143-154.

Agbonifor, B.A. (1998), "The Business Enterprises in Nigeria", Lagos, Longman.

Akhtar, S., R. Raees and M.R. Salaria (2011), "The Impact of Firm, Location and Ownership Specific Factors on Foreign Market Performance of Pakistani SMEs", International Conference on Technology and Business Management, March 28-30, 5132-5521.

Ariyo, D. (2008), "Small Firms are the Backbone of the Nigerian Economy", Africa Economic Analysis, *Academy of Management Journal*, 1(1): 109-124.

Australian Bureau of Statistics (1996), "Industry Wide Statistics", Australia.

Baptista, R., V. Escaria and P. Madruga (2005), "Entrepreneurship, Regional Development and Job Creation: Case for Portugal", Discussion papers on Entrepreneurship, Growth and Public

Policy No. 0605, Max Planck Institute for Research into Economic Systems Group Entrepreneurship, Growth and Public Policy.

Bargal, H., M. Dashmishra and A. Sharma (2009), "Performance Analysis of Small Scale Industries: A Study of Pre-Liberalization and Post-Liberalization Period", *International Journal of Business and Management*, 1(2): 17-26.

Beck, T., Asli Demirguc-Kunt and Ross Levine (2005), "SMEs, Growth, and Poverty: Cross-Country Evidence", *Journal of Economic Growth*, 10(3): 199-229.

Bhati, S.S. (2002), "India: The Role of Small-Scale Industries in an Emerging Economy", in C. Harvie and B.C. Lee (eds.), 'Sustaining SME Innovation, Competitiveness and Development in the Global Economy', July 12-13, 1-18.

Bhutta, M.K., S. Rana and U. Asad (2008), "Owner Characteristics and Health of SMEs in Pakistan", *Journal of Small Business and Enterprise Development*, 15(1): 130-149.

BPS and KUKM (2003), "Indikator Makro Ekonomi Usaha Kecil dan Menengah Tahun", *Berita Resmi Statistik*, 7(21), 1-7.

CACCI (2003), "Recommendations on SME Development for Submission to the APEC Business Advisory Council (ABAC)", available at: www.cacci.org.tw/2003%20Vol%201/CACCI%20Recommendations%20on%20SME%20to%20ABAC.pdf.

Dickey, D.A. and W.A. Fuller (1981), "Likelihood Ratio Statistics for Autoregressive Time Series", *Econometrica,* 49(4): 1057-1072.

Dickey, D.A. and W.A. Fuller (1979), "Distribution for Estimators for Autoregressive Time Series with a Unit Root", *Journal of the American Statistical Society,* 74(366): 427-431.

Feeney, L.S. and A.L. Riding (1997), "Business Owner's Fundamental Trade-off, Finance and the Vicious Circle of Growth and Control", Canadian Business Owners.

Fida, B.A. (2008), "The Importance of Small and Medium Enterprises (SMEs) in Economic Development", Free Online Library.

Fritsch, M. and P. Mueller (2005), "The Persistence of Regional New Business Formation Activity over Time-Assessing the Potential of Policy Promotion Programs", Discussion papers on Entrepreneurship, Growth and Public Policy No. 0205, Max Planck Institute for Research into Economic Systems Group Entrepreneurship, Growth and Public Policy.

Garg, C.C. (1996), "Growth of Small Scale Industries in India: Some Policy Issues", Working Paper No. 10, National Institute of Public Finance and Policy, New Delhi, India.

Garikai, B.W. (2011), "Exportation Challenges by Small and Medium Enterprises and Possible Exportation Strategies", available at: https://www.articlebase.com/business-4056101.html.

GoI (2016), "MSMEs at a Glance", Ministry of Micro, Small and Medium Enterprises, Government of India, New Delhi.

Green, C.J., P. Kimuyu, R. Manos and V. Murinde (2002), "How Do Small Firms in Developing Countries Raise Capital? Evidence from a Large-Scale Survey of Kenyan Micro and Small Scale Enterprises (MSES)", Finance and Development Research Program Working Paper Series No 47, Institute for Development Policy and Management, University of Manchester, Manchester.

Gujarati, D. (2007), "Basic Econometrics", Tata McGraw-Hill Education, 3rd edition, 396-449.

Hameed, A. (2003), "Performance of District Industries Centres in Kerala: An Application of Augmented Solow Model", Ph.D Thesis of the Department of Applied Economics, Cochin University of Science and Technology, Cochin.

Hansen, Bruce E. (1992), "Tests for Parameter Instability in Regressions with I(1) Processes", *Journal of Business and Economic Statistics,* 10(3): 321-335.

Hill, H. (2001), "Small and Medium Enterprises in Indonesia: Old Policy Challenges for a New Administration", *Asian Survey,* 41(2): 248-270.

Indarti, N. and M. Langenberg (2004), "Factors Affecting Business Success among SMEs: Empirical Evidences from Indonesia", Proceedings of the Second Bi-Annual European Summer University 2004, University of Twente, Enschede, The Netherlands.

Johansen, S. (1988), "Statistical Analysis of Co-integration Vectors", *Journal of Economic Dynamics and Control*, 12(2-3): 231-254.

Johansen, S. (1989), "The Power of the Likelihood Ratio Test for Co-integration", Institute of Mathematical Statistics, University of Copenhagen, (Mimeographed).

Johansen, S. (1991), "Estimation and Hypothesis Testing of Co-integration Vectors in Gaussian Vector Autoregressive Models", *Econometrics,* 59(6): 1551-1580.

Johansen, S. (1995), "Likelihood-Based Inference in Co-integrated Vector Autoregressive Models", Oxford: Oxford University Press.

Johansen, S. and K. Jusellius (1990), "Maximum Likelihood Estimation and Inference on Co-integration with Applications to the Demand for Money", *Oxford Bulletin of Economics and Statistics,* 52(2): 169-210.

Kapoor, K., D. Mugwara and I. Chidavaenzi (1997), "Empowering Small Entrepreneurs in Zimbabwe", World Bank Discussion Paper No. 379, Washington D.C.: The World Bank.

Katua, N.T. (2014), "The Role of SMEs in Employment Creation and Economic Growth in Selected Countries", *International Journal of Education and Research*, 2(12): 461-472.

Katyal, A., and B. Xaviour (2015), "A Study on MSMEs' Role in Propelling Economic Development of India and a Discussion on Current HR Issues in MSMEs in India", *International Journal of Scientific and Research Publications*, 5(2): 1-11.

Kotey, B. and G.G. Meredith (1997), "Relationships among Owner/Manager Personal Values, Business Strategies, and Enterprise Performance", *Journal of Small Business Management*, 32(2): 37-64.

Lakshmi, S.P. (2013), "The Performance of Small-Scale Industries in India", *Facts for You*, December, 9-12.

Lied, H.C., M. McPherson and E. Chuta (1994), "Small Enterprise Employment Growth in Rural Africa", *American Journal of Agricultural Economics*, 76(5): 1177-1182.

Lloyd, H.R. (2002), "Small and Medium Enterprises (SMEs): Instruments of Economic Growth and Development in a South African Regional Dispensation", *Discussion Paper*, European Regional Science Association, available at: https://core.ac.uk/download/pdf/7051587.pdf.

Malik, M.A., I.A. Khan, S.A. Bhutto and A.M. Ghouri (2011), "Managerial Skills and Organizational Learning in SMEs of Pakistan", *Indian Journal of Commerce & Management Studies*, 2(4): 60-68.

McDade, B.E. and A. Spring (2005), "The New Generation of African Entrepreneurs: Networking to Change the Climate for Business and Private Sector Led Development", *Entrepreneurship and Regional Development*, 17(1): 17-42.

McPherson, M.A. (1996), "Growth of Micro and Small Enterprises in

Southern Africa", *Journal of Economic Development*, 48(2): 253-277.

Muragia, I. (2008), "Factors that Determine Entrepreneurial Behaviour in Micro and Small Enterprises (MSEs) in Kenya", Nairobi: Scangraphics Ltd.

Muritala, T.A., A.M. Awolaja and Y.A. Bako (2012), "Impact of Small and Medium Enterprises on Economic Growth and Development", *American Journal of Business and Management*, 1(1): 18-22.

Neck, R.E. and Dockner (1987), "Conflict and Cooperation in a Model of Stabilization Policies: A Differential Game Approach", *Journal of Economic Dynamics and Control*, 11(2): 153-159.

Omar, S., L. Arokiasamy and M. Ismail (2009), "The Background and Challenges Faced by the Small Medium Enterprises: A Human Resource Development Perspective", *International Journal of Business and Management,* 4(10): 95-102.

Perks, S. (2004), "The Entrepreneurial Skills Necessary for Growth of Micro Entrepreneurs: An Empirical Study", Proceedings of the International Conference on Entrepreneurship in Africa: Sustainable Globalization, Tshwane University of Technology, Pretoria.

Rajan, K. (2013), "Globalization and Small Scale Industries in India", *International Journal of Advanced Research in Management and Social Sciences*, 2(7): 1-12.

Rajput, N., A. Rajput, G. Batra and S. Oberoi (2012), "Relationship of Exports, Forex and MSMEs in India: An Econometric Study", *Problems and Perspectives in Management*, 10(3): 23-34.

Sen, A. (1980), "Labour and Technology", in J. Cody, H. Hughes and D. Wall (eds.), 'Policies for Industrial Progress in Developing Countries', Oxford, Oxford University Press.

Singh, H., R.K. Singh, R.K. T. Singh (2015), "Small Business Management-Challenges and Road of Opportunities: An Indian Perspective", *International Journal of Science Technology and Management*, 4(2): 11-15.

SMIDEC (2008), "Promoting Innovation-led and Technology-driven SMEs", Paper presented in Asia-Pacific Conference of Technology and Technology Entrepreneurship.

Stel, A.J. Van and K. Suddle (2005), "The Impact of New Firm Formation on Regional Development in the Netherlands", ERIM Report Series ERS-2005-075-ORG, Erasmus Research Institute of Management, Rotterdam.

Stock, James H. and Mark Watson (1993), "A Simple Estimator of Co-integrating Vectors in Higher Order Integrated Systems", *Econometrica*, 61(4): 783-820.

Susmitha M.M. (2014), "Growth and Performance of Small-Scale Industries in India with Special Reference to Kerala", *Facts for You*, April, 15-18.

Tirkey, M.R. (2012), "Role of Micro, Small and Medium Enterprises in Emerging Indian Economy", *Global Journal of Arts and Management*, 2(1): 87-89.

Uma, P. (2013), "Role of SMEs in Economic Development of India", *Asia Pacific Journal of Marketing and Management Review*, 2(6): 120-126.

UNCTAD (2001), "Improving the Competitiveness of SMEs in Developing Countries", United Nations, United Nations Conference on Trade and Development, UNCTAD/ITE/TEB/Misc.3, New York and Geneva.

Wijewardena, H. and G.E. Tibbits (1999), "Factors Contributing to the Growth of Small Manufacturing Firms: Data from Australia", *Journal of Small Business Management*, 37(2): 88-95.

6

Micro, Small and Medium Enterprises: Priceless Diamonds Craving for Polishing

Andrew Francis and J. Vinoth Kumar

Introduction

The role of micro, small and medium enterprises (MSMEs) in the economic and social development of the country is well established. The MSME sector is a nursery of entrepreneurship, often driven by individual creativity and innovation. This sector contributes 8 percent of the country's GDP, 45 percent of the manufactured output and 40 percent of its exports. The MSMEs provide employment to about 60 million people through 26 million enterprises. The labour to capital ratio in MSMEs and the overall growth in the MSME sector is much higher than the large industries.

Compared to many other industries, the geographic distribution of the MSMEs is more even paving the way for balanced growth. Thus, MSMEs are important for the national objectives of growth with equity and inclusion. Needless to say, that the micro, small and medium enterprises sector contribute significantly to the manufacturing output, employment and exports of the country. Further, this sector has consistently registered a higher growth rate than the rest of the industrial sector. There are over 8,000 products ranging from traditional to high-tech items, which are being manufactured by the MSMEs in India. It is well-known that the MSMEs provide the maximum opportunities for both self-employment and jobs after agriculture.

The MSME sector in India is highly heterogeneous in terms of the size of the enterprises, variety of products and services produced and the levels of technology employed. While one end of the MSME spectrum contains highly innovative and high growth enterprises, more than 94 percent of MSMEs are unregistered, with a large number established in the informal or unorganized sector. Besides the growth potential of the sector and its critical role in the manufacturing and value chains, the heterogeneity and the unorganized nature of the Indian MSMEs are important aspects that need to be factored into policy making and programme implementation.

Micro, small and medium enterprises, including khadi and village/rural enterprises are credited with generating the highest rates of employment growth and account for a major share of industrial production and exports. They also play a key role in the development of economies with their effective, efficient, flexible and innovative entrepreneurial spirit. The socio-economic policies adopted by India since the Industries (Development and Regulation) Act, 1951 have laid stress on MSMEs as a means to improve the country's economic conditions.

Majority of people living in rural areas draw their livelihood from agriculture and allied sectors. However, the growth and balanced development of other sectors such as industry and services is also necessary to sustain the growth of Indian economy in an inclusive manner. The Government of India is striving to improve the economic and social conditions of rural population and non-farm sector through a host of measures. This sort of efforts include creation of productive employment opportunities based on optimal use of local raw materials and skills as well as undertaking interventions aimed at improving supply chain, enhancing skills, upgrading technology, expanding markets and capacity building of the entrepreneurs/artisans and their groups.

Current Definition of MSMEs

In India, the enterprises have been classified broadly into two categories: (i) manufacturing and (ii) those engaged in providing/rendering of services.

Both categories of enterprises have been further classified into micro, small and medium enterprises based on their investment in plant and machinery (for manufacturing enterprises) or on equipments (in case of enterprises providing or rendering services). The classification on the basis of investment is given in Table 6.1.

Table 6.1: Classification of MSMEs in India

Categories	Manufacturing (Investment in plant and machinery)	Services (Investment in equipments)
Micro	Does not exceed ₹ 25 lakh	Does not exceed ₹ 10 lakh
Small	More than ₹ 25 lakh but does not exceed ₹ 5 crore	More than ₹ 10 lakh but does not exceed ₹ 2 crore
Medium	More than ₹ 5 crore but does not exceed ₹ 10 crore	More than ₹ 2 crore but does not exceed ₹ 5 crore

Source: Annual Report of MSMEs, 2015-16.

In India, MSME's account for more than 80 percent of total number of industrial enterprises and employ over 6 crore people. As per the estimates and statistics, out of 26 million MSMEs, only 1.5 million are registered and remaining are unregistered. The state-wise distribution of MSMEs is not equal because 55 percent of the MSMEs are in 6 states only, namely, Uttar Pradesh, Maharashtra, Tamil Nadu, West Bengal, Andhra Pradesh and Karnataka. Further, women own about 7 percent of MSMEs and more than 94 percent of the MSMEs are proprietorships or partnerships.

Fast changing global economic scenario has thrown up various opportunities and challenges for the MSMEs in India. While on the one hand, many opportunities have been initiated for this sector to enhance productivity and consider new markets at the national and international level, it has also, on the other hand, put an obligation to upgrade their competencies to meet the competition as new products are launched at a rapid pace and are available worldwide within a very short time. Micro, small and medium enterprises do not have any strategic tools/means for their business/market development as available with large industries. In the present competitive age, marketing is one of the weakest areas wherein MSMEs face major problems.

Marketing, a strategic tool for business development, is critical for the growth and survival of micro, small and medium enterprises. Marketing is the most important factor for the success of any enterprise. Large enterprises have enough resources at their command to hire manpower to take care of marketing of their products and services. MSME sector does not have these resources at their command and thus needs institutional support for providing these inputs in the area of marketing.

Ministry of Micro, Small and Medium Enterprises, inter-alia, through National Small Industries Corporation (NSIC), a public sector enterprise of the Ministry, has been providing marketing support to micro and small enterprises under Marketing Assistance Scheme. Emergence of a large and diverse services sector in the past years had created a situation in which it was no longer enough to address the concerns of the micro and small enterprises (MSEs)—erstwhile known as small-scale industries (SSIs)—alone but essential to include the entire gamut of enterprises, covering both MSE sector and related service entities, in a seamless web. There was a need to provide space for the small enterprises to grow into medium scale enterprises, for that is how they will be able to adopt better and higher levels of technology and remain competitive in a fast globalizing world.

Thus, as in most developed and developing countries, it was necessary that in India too, the concerns of the entire range of enterprises—micro, small and medium—were addressed and the sector was provided with a single legal framework. The Micro, Small and Medium Enterprises Development (MSMED) Act, 2006 addresses these issues and also other issues relating to credit, marketing, technology upgradation etc., concerning the micro, small and medium enterprises. The enactment of MSMED Act, 2006, from October 2, 2006 has brought medium scale industries and service related enterprises also under the purview of this Ministry.

The need of the hour presently is to provide sustenance and support to the whole MSME sector (including service sector), with special emphasis on rural and micro enterprises, through suitable measures to strengthen them for converting the challenges into opportunities and scaling new heights. Thus, although the medium enterprises have also been included as the target beneficiaries under the Scheme, special attention should be given to marketing of products and services of micro and small enterprises, in rural as well as urban areas.

The Government of India, after long deliberations, has come out with well thought out objectives for the marketing of various goods and services offered by MSMEs. If we go through the objectives, we will understand the importance of the role of marketing for the growth of MSMEs. Outlined below are the objectives.

Objectives

1. To enhance marketing capabilities and competitiveness of the MSMEs.
2. To showcase the competencies of MSMEs.
3. To update MSMEs about the prevalent market scenario and its impact on their activities.
4. To facilitate the formation of consortia of MSMEs for marketing of their products and services.
5. To provide platform to MSMEs for interaction with large institutional buyers.
6. To disseminate/propagate various programmes of the Government.
7. To enrich the marketing skills of the micro, small and medium entrepreneurs.

Strategy

After defining the objectives, the Government of India also outlines various strategies to make MSMEs expand their scope and reach, while also ensuring that every unit is a viable and vibrant one. They are as under:

Organizing International Technology Exhibitions in Foreign Countries by NSIC and Participation in International Exhibitions/Trade Fairs with a view to providing broader exposure to Indian micro, small and medium enterprises to facilitate them in exploring new business opportunities in emerging and developing markets. These exhibitions are organized in consultation with the concerned stakeholders and industry associations etc. The calendar for these events are finalized well in advance and publicized widely amongst all participants/stakeholders. The calendar of events is also displayed on the website of NSIC. Such expositions showcase the diverse technologies, products and services produced/rendered by Indian MSMEs and provide them with excellent business opportunities, besides promoting trade, establishing joint ventures, technology transfers, marketing arrangements and image building of Indian MSMEs in foreign countries.

In addition to the organisation of the international exhibitions, NSIC also facilitates participation of Indian MSMEs in select international exhibitions and trade fairs. Participation in such events exposes MSMEs to international practices and enhances their business prowess. These events provide a platform to MSMEs where they meet, discuss, and conclude agreements on technical and business collaborations.

Organizing Theme-based Domestic Exhibitions and Technology Fairs and Participation in Exhibitions/Trade Fairs in India in order to provide marketing opportunities to MSMEs within the country, with focus on products and services offered by MSMEs, including technologies suitable for employment generation, products from specific regions or clusters (like North-Eastern region). Micro, small and medium enterprises are provided space at concessional rates to exhibit their products and services at such exhibitions/fairs. Apart from the above, NSIC also facilitates participation of MSMEs in exhibitions/trade fairs/events being organized by various State Government departments, industry associations and other institutions all over the country to exhibit their products and services. These exhibitions are organised in consultation with the concerned stakeholders and industry associations etc. Participation in such events is expected to help MSMEs in enhancing their marketing avenues by way of capturing new markets and expanding the existing markets. This would also help them in becoming ancillaries, partners in joint ventures and sub-contracting for large companies.

NSIC has been organising Techmart exhibition every year during the India International Trade Fair (IITF) in the month of November. This is an international exhibition showcasing the best MSME products, technologies and services of India. A minimum of up to 30 percent of the total area is normally allocated for the entrepreneurs belonging to the Special Category i.e. entrepreneurs belonging to North-East region/women and SC/ST category. The subsidy is available on space charges for the special category MSMEs.

Support for Co-sponsoring of Exhibitions organized by other organizations/industry associations/agencies is provided to various institutions, industry associations and organizations engaged in promotion and development of MSMEs, for organizing exhibitions/fairs within the country for the benefit of the MSME sector. This support is provided in the form of co-sponsoring of the events by NSIC.

In order to apply for co-sponsoring of an event by NSIC, the applicant organization/agency has to fulfil certain criteria/conditions.

Buyer-Seller Meets are organized to bring bulk buyers/ Government departments and micro, small and medium enterprises together under one platform. Bulk and departmental buyers such as the Railways, Defence, Communication departments and large companies are invited to participate in buyer-seller meets to bring them closer to the MSMEs for enhancing their marketing competitiveness. These programmes are aimed at vendor developments from micro, small and medium enterprises for the bulk buyers. Participation in these programmes enables MSMEs to know the requirements of bulk buyers on the one hand and help the bulk buyers to know the capabilities of MSMEs for their purchases. These buyers-seller meets are organized in consultation with the concerned stakeholders, including industry associations and other agencies involved in industrial development.

Intensive Campaigns and Marketing Promotion Events are conducted all over the country to disseminate information about the various schemes for the benefit of micro, small and medium enterprises. They are also facilitated to enrich their knowledge regarding latest developments, quality standards etc. and improve the marketing potential of their products and services.

Other than the above, certain activities are undertaken for supporting the marketing efforts of MSMEs like:

- Development of display centres, show windows and hoardings etc. for promoting products and services of MSMEs,
- Printing of literature, brochures and product-specific catalogues and CDs etc. and preparation of short films for disseminating information,
- Development of website/portal for facilitating the marketing of MSME products and services,
- Development and dissemination of advertising and publicity material about various programmes/schemes for MSME sectors and events,
- Preparation and upgradation of MSME manufacturers/ suppliers/exporters directory,
- Documentation of the success stories of MSMEs,
- Conducting studies to explore and assess new markets/businesses and product ranges for both domestic and International markets, and

- Hosting international delegations and networking events.

Benefits for MSMEs

The various benefits the MSMEs can reap because of the marketing strategies can be enumerated as follows:

1. Enhanced marketing capabilities and competitiveness of the MSMEs.
2. Platform to showcase the competencies of MSMEs.
3. Exposure to prevalent market scenario and its impact on their activities.
4. Encouraging formation of consortia of MSMEs for marketing of their products and services.
5. Platform to MSMEs for interaction with large institutional buyers.
6. Getting apprised about various programmes of the Government.
7. Enrichment of the marketing skills of the micro, small and medium entrepreneurs.
8. Financial assistance by way of providing subsidy on space rent, airfare and freight charges.
9. Exposure to international best practices and latest technology and global buyers.
10. Export opportunities and business expansion.

Financial Assistance under the Scheme

The applications/proposals for seeking assistance under the scheme shall be submitted directly to NSIC, with full details and justification. The consolidated proposal shall be put up before the Screening Committee, set up under Para 6 of the scheme, for consideration. The Screening Committee shall examine and consider the proposals, keeping in view the eligibility conditions and other criteria laid down under the scheme. While processing the proposals, preference shall be given to participants/units who have not availed of the benefits under this scheme or other such schemes of the Ministry earlier. The proposals, after processing by the screening committee, shall be put up for approval by the chairman-cum-managing director of NSIC along with its recommendations. The proposals requiring approval of the Administrative Ministry shall be forwarded by CMD, NSIC, with proper justification, for consideration and approval of the Ministry, in consultation with IFD. The assistance shall be released by NSIC to the concerned applicant organization on reimbursement basis on receipt of the event report and other prescribed documents, including feedback from the participants.

Achievements

NSIC has facilitated participation of around 716 MSMEs by organizing 8 international level exhibitions:

1. India Manufacturing Show, 2014, Bangalore (Karnataka);
2. Techmart India, 2014, New Delhi (Inaugurated by Hon'ble Union Minister for MSMEs);
3. Imphal Expo, 2014, Imphal (Manipur);
4. 2nd Edition of Soumex, 2014, Chennai (Tamil Nadu);
5. 7th Vibrant Gujarat, Gandhi Nagar (Gujarat);
6. DICCI Industrial and Trade Expo, 2015 Hyderabad (Andhra Pradesh);
7. International Trade Fair, Guwahati (Inaugurated by Hon'ble Union Minister for MSMEs); and
8. Shillong International Trade Fair, Shillong (Meghalaya).

1,235 MSMEs from across the country were also facilitated for participation in 117 domestic exhibitions held in various part of country. In addition, 167 MSMEs were supported to exhibit their products in 12 foreign exhibitions held in the countries like US, Israel, Kenya, Dubai, South Africa, Japan, Sri Lanka, Slovenia, Korea, Turkey, Russia and Chile. 12 buyer-seller meets and 635 marketing workshops/campaigns were conducted during the year for supporting marketing efforts of MSME.

Major Problems of MSMEs

Despite its commendable contribution to the nation's economy, MSME Sector does not get the required support from the concerned Government departments, banking sector, financial institutions and corporate sector, which is a handicap in their becoming more competitive in the national and international markets and which needs to be taken up for immediate and proper redressal. MSME sector faces a number of problems—absence of adequate and timely bank finance, limited knowledge and non-availability of suitable technology, low production capacity, follow up with various agencies in solving regular activities and lack of interaction with government agencies on various matters.

The MSME sector is one of the greatest contributors in domestic production as well as export earnings. Many major mergers have taken place recently. But MSMEs face a host of problems that make them cripple and curtail their activities and output. They are described below.

Financial Problems: Finance is the life blood of any business. The financial problem of MSMEs is the root cause for all other problems faced by the MSME sector. The small and medium entrepreneurs generally have a limited budget and there are no facilities for cheap credit. They fall into the clutches of money lender who charge very high rates of interest, or else they borrow from the dealers of their goods, who exploit them by compelling them to sell their products at very low price. After the Nationalization of 14 major Indian banks in July 1969, the commercial banks were catering to only a small proportion of SMEs. Credit to the MSME sector continues to be non-commensurate with its contribution to the total industrial output. As against the share of the village and MSME at 40 percent in the industrial output, their share in total credit to the industrial sector is only about 30 percent.

Non-availability of Raw Material: This difficulty is experienced in a very pronounced form. The quantity, quality and regularity of the supply of raw material is not satisfactory. There are no quantity discounts, since they are purchased in small quantities and hence charged at higher prices by the suppliers. Difficulty is also experienced in procuring semi-manufactured materials. Financial weakness stands in the way of securing raw materials in bulk in a competitive market.

Production Problems: MSME units suffer from inadequate work space, power, lighting and ventilation, and safety measures etc. These shortcomings have tended to endanger the health of workmen and have adversely affected the rate of production. Many units are following primitive methods of production. Adoption of modern techniques is either disliked by the entrepreneurs or is not feasible. Wage rates and service conditions of small industries are not attractive to skilled labour.

Lack of Appropriate and Up-to-date Technology: Today, technology is changing at a very fast pace; it becomes difficult for MSMEs to cope up with changing technology. Technology up gradation and the frequent need to renew the equipment has emerged as a big problem.

Marketing: Next to finance, marketing is the most vital aspect of any business activity. As marketing is not properly organized for MSMEs, the helpless artisans are completely at the mercy of the middle men. The potential demand for their goods remains underdeveloped. The MSMEs have to face the competition from large scale units in marketing their products. It causes damage to the growth and stability of MSMEs. MSMEs cannot afford to spend lavishly on advertisements to promote their sales.

Managerial Problem: Small-scale industries in our country have suffered from the lack of entrepreneurial ability to develop initiative and undertake risks in the unexplored industrial fields. The inefficiency in management comes first among managerial problems. The entrepreneurial ability of promoters of cottage industries and MSMEs are handicapped by technical know-how in the areas of production, finance, accounting and marketing management.

Sickness of MSMEs: A serious problem which is hampering small and medium sector has been the sickness. Many small units have fallen sick due to one problem or the other. Sickness is caused by two sets of factors—internal and external. From among the various internal and external causes of sickness, the important ones are bud management, high rate of capital gearing, inadequacy of finance, shortage of raw material, outdated plant and machinery, low labour productivity etc.

Lack of Storage and Warehousing facilities: Another important problem of the MSMEs is the lack of storage and warehousing facilities. The goods produced, especially the perishable commodities, require proper warehousing and storage facilities. Lack of storage and warehousing facilities brings huge loss because they have to be sold at a nominal price as they cannot wait for a better price.

Suggestions

MSMEs need to be helped and supported for the growth of the economy and for the well-being of the poorer sections of the society who are engaged in MSME activities. Hence, we propose a few suggestions for making the MSME sector more active, agile and vibrant:

1. The government needs to organize more trade fairs for the entrepreneurs.
2. The Ministry should conduct more training programmes for the entrepreneurs.
3. The Ministry needs to develop innovative channels for marketing. The advertisement and sales promotion strategy needs to improve.
4. The trade fair advertisements sometimes do not reach the rural entrepreneurs in time.
5. Storage and warehousing facility for the MSMEs should be provided at war footing to avoid wastages. This will also enable the MSMEs to fix a reasonable price for their products both in the lean period and in the peak season.

Conclusion

To conclude, the MSME sector of India is today at the gateway of global growth on the strength of competitive and quality product range. However, facilitation from the Government is required to minimize the transaction costs of technology upgradation, market penetration, modernization of infrastructure etc. There should be proper market research and development with respect to the innovative methods of production and service rendering.

The MSME sector has habitually been termed the 'engine of growth' for budding economies. Over the last few years, there has been major policy changes at the national and state level aimed at consolidating this emerging sector. Poor infrastructure and insufficient market linkages are among key factors that have restricted the growth of the MSMEs sector. Lack of ample and appropriate access to finance has continued to be the biggest challenge.

References

Ali, Anis and Firoz Husain (2014), "MSME'S in India: Problems, Solutions and Prospectus in Present Scenario", *International Journal of Engineering and Management Sciences*, Vol. 5(2), 109-115.

"Annual Report, 2015-16", Ministry of Micro, Small and Medium Enterprises, Government of India, New Delhi.

"MSME Development Act, 2006", Ministry of Micro, Small and Medium Enterprises, Government of India, New Delhi.

Syal, Subina, "Role of MSMEs in the Growth of Indian Economy", *Global Journal of Commerce and Management Perspective*, Vol. 55), 40-43.

7

Internationalization and Innovation in Indian SMEs: A Study of Indian IT Sector

Rushi Pandya and Ashutosh Muduli

Introduction

Internationalization has continued to be a popular step for a large number of firms in the world. In this trend of going global, small and medium scale enterprises (SMEs) have also gained benefits of fading barriers of borders (Morkertaite and Sekliuckiene, 2015). Globalization and liberalization of economies has provided a large number of opportunities for SMEs and start-ups to grow. SMEs from developing countries have also expanded into international markets.

Growth by diversification in international markets helps the organization to increase their revenues due to a large number of customers. The process of innovation and its management can improve their chance of success but that includes a higher investment risk (Andersson and Helander, 2009).

Small firms do not have enough resources to follow all the strategic steps for internationalization. Small companies are required to develop the strategies to utilize all the available resources to its optimum levels. It gives them an opportunity to innovate. Innovation and its management can become their competitive advantage and core competency in the market to become a large successful organization.

Research has also tried to touch upon organizations' internal and external challenges for managing innovation with internationalization. It has also proposed a model for SMEs and start-ups to balance innovation and internationalization.

Internationalization for SMEs and Start-ups

In modern management research, the term internationalization has been used frequently by research scholars and academicians. The term was explained by the scholars of Australia and published with much elaboration in research publications (Ruzzier, Hisrich and Antoncic, 2006). Internationalization has been a very important step for the organizations regardless of their size. It is defined as an opportunity to exploit newer markets with core competencies of the organization (Lu, Beamish and Paul, 2001).

In the last decade, SMEs have shown growth and contributed a lot to the world economy by inculcating internationalization strategies and practices. For example, 99 percent of the organizations in the European Union are SMEs (Europen Commission , 2015) and 90 percent of Indian industry units are SMEs (B2B information, 2013).

SMEs have become a very important part of the Indian economy where 50 percent of exports are from SMEs. SMEs are expected to rise at an annual growth rate of 8 percent. Many SMEs from India have expanded their services and products to different countries.

Most of the SMEs are integrating internationalization by developing import-export units in one or more countries (Pereira, 2013). SMEs also have adopted a practice of partnership and joint ventures to establish their organizations in other countries. Collaborating with other organizations can help the Indian SMEs to learn and develop new knowledge base which can be used to improve products and services provided by them in the foreign markets.

Need for Internationalization

Much of the information technology SMEs based in India have explored new countries as their potential markets. They have experimented in different ways to provide services to potential customers. Partnering with regional companies for entering into that market is the largely observed method adopted by start-ups and SMEs (Athreye and Kapur, 2009). Indian IT companies are always looking for opportunities in the developed economies to expand their digital products and services. The international market is always a preferred market by technology SMEs, as it provides a large number of potential customers and possibly higher revenues.

The internet has eliminated the concept of distance for the development of IT-based projects. Using this advantage, SMEs can afford to open business branches in other countries with development centers in India. It has made internationalization easier as well as affordable for small and medium scale enterprises (Coviello and Munro, 1995).

Internationalization is seen as an advantage for transfer of capital, labor, and technology in new geography as market creates lots of opportunities to learn about the latest technology, economy, and market. Collaborating with other companies can help to acquire new expertise which can assist in strengthening an organization's position.

Internationalization is the process to see beyond domestic markets. It allows the organization to understand the global trends and markets. SMEs can learn the latest practices to be in competition in international markets with growth-oriented strategy and to serve a large number of potential customers from foreign markets (Osarenkhoe, 2008). It also helps the organization to innovate for competition with other international organizations.

In the field of information technology, start-ups and SMEs are considered as reputed organizations if they have a strong technology base and global presence. A good global reputation of an organization is very important for its sustainable growth (Athreye and Kapur, 2009). Internationalization for IT-based SMEs is very important and it is inevitable in the current competitive economic conditions and globalization.

Challenges for Internationalization

Internationalization is a practice to expand services and

products into international markets where there is a need and scope for acceptance amongst a large user base (Theocharakis, 2014). SMEs adopting internationalization face many challenges during the entire process of internationalization. These challenges are listed under the following headings.

How to Select a New Market? SMEs and start-ups take the process of internationalization to find new customers for their services and products. Information technology products and services have an advantage that it does not require large capital funds to establish new facilities in different markets (McDougall and Oviate, 1994). It requires basic infrastructure which can be set up at a moderate cost in any part of the world.

Selecting a new international market is the most important challenge for SMEs. Denis and Papadopoulos (1987) suggest that international market selection should be based on a systematic approach. Root's (1987) model has emphasized on a data-driven approach about estimating the market size and its potential customers.

Selecting the right international market is also dependent on external factors like economic policies, stability and business environment of the target country. Wrong market selection can dearly cost an organization and can affect its core business strategy (Matenge and Tendy, 2011).

In a majority of SMEs and start-ups, the decision of selection of market is based on 'non-systematic approach'. 'Opportunistic' approach is adopted by organizations considering weaker administrative capacities for market analysis and research. It is found that lack of international managerial experience also affects the decision of selecting new international markets.

Globalization has helped IT-based companies for easy access to information about new markets but it always needs skills and experience for selection and implementation of the new international market strategy.

How to Manage the Technology Competency? Advanced technology, new product capability, and responsiveness to the market change are the key core competencies of technology based new ventures. IT-based start-ups and SMEs with their products and services need higher responsiveness according to the market needs for successful internationalization. Internationalization of technology ventures affects the technological capability and innovations (Ribeiro, Jr., Borini and Bernardes, 2014).

It is important to adopt appropriate technological changes and strategies which can help the process of internationalization. On responsive technological changes, an organization can maximize their revenues by providing solutions to international customers. It requires an approach beyond the local markets and understanding of the global market needs.

To adapt to the changes and the highly responsive strategies, start-ups and SMEs do not have extra resources and excess of capital funds to invest in specialized technological advancements. It requires a thorough understanding of the consumer needs and current business practices.

Partnering with the existing companies in the international market can be an inviting step but there should be proper business terms between both the parties which should help the organization to learn and perform with flexibility and efficiency.

How to Design Strategies for Internationalization? In India, there are two types of start-ups and SMEs in the field of information technology. First is 'an Uppsala model firm or traditional firms'—organizations which have a stronghold in the domestic markets and which have gradually moved to international markets. The other is 'Born global' organizations who have designed their strategies only by considering the international markets since their inception (Ruzzier, Hisrich and Antoncic, 2006).

Uppsala model firms were started with the strategies to work in the domestic markets. They have a good hold in the domestic market with sound technical ability to meet the demands. Gradually, with capacity building and by understanding the saturation in the domestic markets, the firm decides to explore the new international markets based on the experiences and available information. This approach is ideally correct but during the implementation stage, entrepreneurs fail to redesign their business model to meet the demands of international customers. They also face challenges in adopting the new practices and introducing new methods in their organization to meet the standards of international markets.

Born global firms are focused on approaching international markets. They have an advantage over the former type. The growth of the organization is much faster than the Uppsala model firms. The major challenge is in terms of capital funds required during the initial stages. To enter into the international market, start-up is required to understand and to practice the international standards and strategies. It also requires competitive and sustainable technical capabilities for international markets.

The observation is that SMEs and start-ups have a big challenge to manage with respect to funds to run different operations inside and outside the organization at the initial stage. Born global firms have to invest more into their different operations to meet the criteria of international markets to compete and earn revenue.

Designing the strategy for internationalizing is a systematic process and it should be implemented with an integrated approach which does not affect the performance of the organization negatively. It should include time of internationalization, target markets, resource utilization and business objectives.

How to Manage People? Organizations are made of people regardless of their size. Founders and employees are the most critical factors for any SMEs and start-ups. Human factor is more important for an international organization. It is essential to understand that the existing philosophy of people management in domestic markets may not work for operations in international markets. SMEs and start-ups must understand the differences between cultures and attributes of people (Muduli, 2015).

International firms compete in an increasingly complex environment where the level of challenge of doing business can be highly variable (Mitchell and Gao, 2009). Adoption of globalized culture, management of knowledge and effective methods of communication should also be given the best resources and investment of efforts by SMEs and start-ups.

Innovation Management for SMEs and Start-ups

In a developing country like India, SMEs are very important for the growth of the economy. Increasingly, SMEs are creating a competitive environment. In such a scenario, hi-tech enterprises have a major challenge ahead to sustain their edge over the market. Technology life cycles and product life cycles are shortening due to cut-throat competition in the market (Tiwari and Buse, 2007).

This changing market, forces SMEs to adopt new strategies and develop new technologies frequently to be in the competition. It is essential for them to reinvent their business models according to the dynamic market needs. Varying business model is considered as inconvenient for the SMEs. Due to limited resources and experiences, SMEs cannot survive in the market without innovating.

Innovation for SMEs is very important as it gives them an edge over the market. Collaboration in between the departments and with other firms can help the SMEs to innovate (Zen, Amal and Santos, 2014). Expanding to different regions and partnering with international firms for resources and technology are important for SMEs' growth. Innovation in different processes provides SMEs a competitive advantage.

IT-based SMEs in India have created a competitive market. Due to this competition, it is inevitable for them to avoid innovation. There are two types of innovation methods that are observed: (i) technology innovation and (ii) business model innovation (Vanhaverbeke, 2012). For technology innovation, SMEs have their in-house technology development cell. New technology provides competitive advantage for the firm. Business model innovation is possible without having in-house technology development facilities. SMEs can leverage from the external technology partners and expand their services (Luggen, 1975).

Innovation is not a once-in-a-while process. It is an approach for consistent growth of the organization to meet the dynamic market needs and stay in competition. Innovation management in IT-based SMEs is an essential part of the organizational processes that improvises the traditional approach for new product development or process development (Cognizant Business Consultancy, 2012).

This inspires exploratory approach and creative thinking. Firms relying on technology-based innovations are required to expand their core competencies and sustain in the market through constant innovations. Similar to business model innovation, organizations need to understand the market needs in "top-bottom" and "bottom-top" approach. It is to understand the industry insights and customer insights respectively.

Innovation management is not only constrained to research and development processes. Innovation also affects an organization's culture. To inculcate the culture of innovation inside an organization is a strategic task which is required for organizational innovation.

New age IT firms are coming up with new approaches to include innovativeness in different processes in their organizations. It also improves the readiness of the organization for new ideas and changes (Tiwari and Buse, 2007). Strategic and disciplined implementation of the innovative processes helps the organization to provide sustainable innovations to the market with consistency.

Challenges of Innovation Management

Start-ups and SMEs are always caught in a dilemma—with

the pressure of competition they are required to perform consistently. Expectations of higher quality by the customers and tighter cost control strategies by SMEs make a practice of innovative processes important. With the limited information about markets and resources of managerial and technical expertise, small businesses are skeptical about implementing the new ideas.

IT-based start-ups and SMEs are growing in India at an exponential pace (NASSCOM, 2014). This increasing growth is a good sign for the economy of the nation. It is also observed that Indian start-ups and SMEs are not competitive when it comes to innovative technology developments. There are internal as well as external challenges for organizations related to management of innovations.

External Challenges

Market Uncertainty: Uncertainty in the global market has affected the needs of SMEs. Marketplaces are changing dynamically. Technology interventions and environment of acceptance of new technology products based on the regional factors have become ambiguous.

There is an ambiguity about the real potential of foreign markets, customer needs and its size due to rapid changes. With compatibility standards for the technology not established, rapid or unpredictable changes tend to follow (Theocharakis, 2014).

Technological Uncertainty: Due to competitive markets, technology life cycles have also become shorter and can be easily replaced by the new alternatives. SMEs need to consider whether their technological solution is providing a good alternative to the customers or not. It is really important to understand the usability of the technology for the different markets.

This is driven by the lack of information about: (i) the reliability of the technology, (ii) the product's functional performance, and (iii) unexpected side-effects. The development of a new technology will obsolete an existing technology and may itself be rapidly become obsolete by a forthcoming technology (Zou, Liu and Ghauri, 2010).

Internal Challenges

Organizational Readiness for Innovations: Technology based start-ups and SMEs have competitive markets globally. The market needs are changing due to alternative solutions and development of new breakthrough technologies. This is important for the organization to understand the changes and include competitive flexibility as their core competency. Readiness for exploratory approach and adopting new practices to replace the existing processes is important for an organization to be competent to innovate.

The majority of SMEs employees and owners are skeptical about taking new ideas and processes into implementation (Razavi and Attarnezhad, 2013). It involves many factors viz., limited funds and knowledge, resources to experiment and infrastructure.

Organizational Change for Innovation Management: Small and medium scale organizations are also finding it challenging to introduce change in the organization with changing markets. Innovation cannot happen in isolation but it is a process of collective efforts by a team of people (Kiran, Majmudar and Kishore, 2010).

Organizations do not introduce change in the organization effectively which weakens the impact of change and it results into ambiguity among the employees (Muduli, 2009). It is also observed that start-ups in India are lacking scalable knowledge management infrastructure. Knowledge management facilities are considered as the base of ideation and innovations (Johanson and Vahlne, 1997).

Internationalization and Innovation Management

In 1776, Adam Smith proposed that international competition was in the best interest of a nation. He quoted "consumption is the sole end purpose of all the production"

(Zen, Amal and Santos, 2014). Internationalization of the firms is essential for the growth of an economy. It helps to expand the business into newer markets and serve a large number of consumers in different geographical locations. IT-based SMEs and start-ups in India have marked their presence in different parts of the world to get a higher number of potential customers (Bhatti and Kumar, 2012).

Most of the companies have selected developed countries as their target market for internationalization. Companies have internationalized using different methods i.e. partnership with local firms, establishing their facilities in other countries and importing and exporting of services and products (Forsman, Hinttu and Kock, 2002).

Internationalization provides start-ups and SMEs an opportunity to expand their reach and cater to new markets. It helps them to leverage the financial resources by serving a whole new segment of customers. Internationalization also helps the organization to increase their technological competencies by partnering with the local firms. It increases the chances of innovation.

New markets and new consumers will challenge firms to innovate. Innovation in the business models and technology according to needs of new markets and customers also increases company's revenues.

However, there are difficulties in the process of innovation in the internationalized firms as regards the transferability of the resources. Different cultures in an organization affect the knowledge sharing process and information flow. Lack of strategic and managerial skills affects innovation management and internationalization. It challenges SMEs and start-ups to select either innovation or internationalization (Chelliah, Sulaiman and Yusoff, 2010).

In technology firms, protection of intellectual property rights is very important to maintain a competitive advantage. Internationalization of a firm can affect the protection of those rights while sharing the resources with other firms to gain larger international markets. It can become a threat to the technological competency of an organization. Partnership terms must include the conditions for sharing and protecting intellectual property rights.

Innovation process and management are very much an integral part of an organization. It requires essential resources to innovate new products and services. SMEs and start-ups who have ventured for late internationalization must redesign their strategies to maintain common organizational goals across all the facilities of the firm.

All the centers of an organization should work to achieve common business goals and objectives. The inefficient organizational communication channel can adversely affect the performances of individual offices. It affects the development and commercialization process of innovative technologies in large markets. Human resources management is also an important aspect which affects successful internationalization and efficient innovation management in an organization.

Hence, internationalization of the SMEs and start-ups is a huge opportunity for them to expand their market reach and to grow faster and in a sustainable way. However, it is also a tough challenge for small and medium scale technology organizations to manage with limited resources.

Conclusion and Scope for Further Research

Indian economy has a high dependence on SMEs and start-ups as they contribute 90 percent of the total industrial firms in the nation. SMEs and start-ups have witnessed the importance of internationalization and leveraged the benefits of globalization to expand into new countries.

Market expansion is a risk for small and medium scale organizations because it utilizes their limited resources to attract a large number of potential customers (Berisha and Lama, 2013). There are challenges involved in internationalization.

It requires a thorough understanding of the new markets

and customer needs. IT-based organizations prefer to expand into developed economies where the product life cycle and technology life cycle is becoming smaller with a competitive global environment. Hence, India based SMEs and start-ups must understand the importance of innovation and its management. Innovation management can give SMEs technological core competencies and can help organizations to succeed in competition.

To be an innovative organization, SMEs and start-ups have to understand the importance of research and development and knowledge management. It is recommended that Indian SMEs should partner with international technology firms for resource sharing.

Developing the culture of innovation and an open communication setup in an organization would help increase the responsiveness of an organization.

Organizational leadership should be effective and efficient to take strategic decisions for the overall growth. It increases the possibilities of successful commercialization of innovative products and services in the international market. The proposed model is based on the available literature and in-depth conversations with concerned people in SMEs and start-ups as regards the challenges faced by them.

The research work can be taken forward to understand the proposed model for SMEs and start-ups in detail. It can provide a solution for technology-based SMEs and start-ups to innovate, while internationalizing successfully.

References

Al-Laham, A. and Souitaris, V. (2008), "Network Embeddedness and New Venture Internationalization:Analyzing International Linkages in the German Biotech Industry", *Journal of Business Venturing*, 567-586.

Andersson, A. and Helander, A. (2009), "The Influence of Network Relationships in the Internationalization of SMEs", available at: http://hj.diva-portal.org/smash/get/diva2:223104/FULLTEXT01.

Athreye, S. and Kapur, S. (2009), "The Internationalization of

Chinese and Indian Firms: Trends, Motivations and Strategy", Birkbeck, London, UK.

B2Binformation (2013), available at: http://b2binformation.blogspot.in/2010/07/how-is-sme-sector-growing-in-india.html.

Berisha, B. And Lama, S. (2013), "Internationalization of SMEs in the Finnish Food Processing Industries", available at: http://www.doria.fi/:http://www.doria.fi/bitstream/handle/10024/93774/501983_501979.pdf?sequence=2.

Bhatti, D.M. and Kumar, D.D. (2012), "Internationalization Factors and Entrepreneurial Perception: Indication from Yemen SMEs",. *Far East Journal of Psychology and Business*.

Brem, A. and Voigt, K.I. (2009), "Innovation Management in Emerging Technology Ventures: The Concept of an Integrated Idea Management", *Internationa Journal of Technology, Policy and Management*, 304-321.

Carlsson, B. (2003), "Internationalization of Innovation Systems: A Survey of the Literature", in Keith Pavitt (ed.), 'What Do We Know About Innovations?', Brighton.

Chelliah, D.S., Sulaiman, D.M. and Yusoff, Y.M. (2010), "Internationalization and Performance: Small and Medium Enterprises in Malaysia", *International Journal of Business and Management*, 27-37.

Cognizant Business Consultancy (2012), "Innovation Beyond the Four Walls: Breaking Down Innovation Barriers", London: Congnizant Business Consultancy.

Coviello, N.E. and Munro, H. (1995), "Growing the Entrepreneurial Firm Networking for International Market Development", *European Journal of Marketing*, 49-61.

Coviello, N.E. and Martin, K.A. (1999), "Internationalization of Service SMEs:An Integrated Perspective from the Engineering Consulting Sector", *Journal of Internationa] Marketing*, 42-67.

Etemad, H. and Ala-Mutka, J. (n.d.), "Growth and Internationalization Strategies of Rapidly Growing and Internationalizing Enterprises from Canada and Finland".

Europen Commission (2015), "Fact and Figures About the EU's Small and Medium Enterprises (SMEs)", available at: http://ec.europa.eu/:http://ec.europa.eu/enterprise/policies/sme/facts-figures-analysis/index_en.htm.

Fatima, S., Rehman, F.U. and Ali, P.D. (2011), "Formation and

Internationalization of IT Firms of Pakistan: A Resource Based View", *Business and Management Review*, 65-81.

Federal Ministry for Economic Cooperation and Development (2012), "Managing Change and Innovation: A Challenge for Modern Organizations", Mannheim, Germany: Deutsche Gesellschaft für Internationale Zusammenarbeit (GIZ) GmbH.

Forsman, M., Hinttu, S. and Kock, S. (2002), "Internationalization from a SME Perspective", Conference paper presented at the IMP Conference in Dijon, France.

Innovation Point (n.d.), "Framework for Strategic Innovation: Blending Strategy and Creative Exploration to Discover the Future Business Opportunity", San Francisco: Innovation Point.

Ishchenko and Marina, P.L. (2013), "The Internationalisation Process of the Smaller Firm: An Examination of the Craft Microenterprise", *Repositório Institucional da Universidade Católica Portuguesa.*

Johanson, J. And Vahlne, J.E. (1997), "The Internationalization Process of the Firm: A Model of Knowledge Development and Increasing Foreign Market Commitments", 23-32.

Kiran, V., Majmudar, M. and Kishore, K. (2010), "Internationalization of SMEs: Finding a Way Ahead", *American International Journal of Research in Humanities, Arts and Social Sciences*, 19-23.

Krasniqi, E. And Kume, A. (2013), "Entrepreneurship and Strategic Management in Emerging Entrepreneurship and Strategic Management", *Annales Universitatis Apulensis Series Oeconomica*, 267-279.

Krasniqi, E. And Kume, A. (2013), "Entrepreneurship and Strategic Management in Emerging Economy", *Annales Universitatis Apulensis Series Oeconomica*, 267-279.

Laghzaoui and Soulaimane (n.d.), "Competencies, Internationalization of SME: A Reading in Terms of Resources", Aix en Provence, France.

Lecerf, M.A. (2012), "Internationalization and Innovation: The Effects of a Strategy Mix on the Economic Performance of French SMEs", *International Business Research*, 1-13.

Lee, J., Lee, J.H. and Choi, B. (2014), "Effects of Internationalization on Innovation in the Service Industry: Evidence from Korea", *Journal of East Asian Economic Integration*, 339-366.

Lu, J.W., Beamish, N. and Paul, P. (2001), "The Internationalization and Performance of SMEs", *Strategic Management Journal*, 565-581.

Luggen, M. (1975), "Technology and Innovation Management in New Technology-Based Firms", Zurich.

Masanell, R.C. and Ricart, J.E. (2009), "Company Strategy: Business Model Reconfiguration for Innovation and Internationalization", Barcelona, Spain.

Matenge and Tendy (2011), "Small Firm Internationalization: A Developing Country Perspective", *International Journal of Business Administration,* Volume 2, 103-111.

McDougall and Oviate (1994), "Towards a Theory of International New Venture", *Journal of International Business Studies*, 45-61.

Mitchell , M. E. And Gao, Y. (2009), "Probe into the Modes of International Human Resource Management in Chinese Small and Medium Enterprises", available at: http://wbiconpro.com/9.Margaretdoc.pdf.

Morkertaite, R. and Sekliuckiene, J. (2015), "Preconditions for Born Global Internationalization: Network Approach", *Social Sciences*.

Muduli, A. (2015), "High Performance Work System, HRD Climate and Organizational Performance: An Empirical Study", *European Journal of Training and Development,* Volume 39, Issue 3, 239-257.

Muduli, A. (2009), "Developing Corporate Entrepreneurship through Achievement Motivation Training: A University Level Study", *The ICFAI Journal of Organisational Behaviour*, Volume 33, Issue 3, 354-372.

NASSCOM (2014), "NASSCOM Annual Report, 2014", New Delhi, India.

OECD (2009), "Top Barriers and Drivers to SME Internationalization", OECD Working Party on SMEs and Entrepreneurship.

Osarenkhoe, A. (2008), "A Study of the Enablers of Non-sequential Internationalization Process among Small and Medium-sized Firms", *Inernational. Journal of Business Science and Applied Management*, 1-20.

Razavi, S.H. and Attarnezhad, O. (2013), "Management of Organizational Innovation" *International Journal of Business and Social Science*, 226-232.

Ribeiro, F.C., F.M. Borini and R. Bernardes (2014), "Accelerated Internationalization in Emerging Markets: Empirical Evidence from Brazilian Technology-Based Firms", *Journal of Technology Management and Innovation*, 1-12.

Ruigrok, W. and H. Wagner (2003), "Internationalization and Performance: An Organizational Learning Perspective", *Management International Review*, 63-83.

Rutashobya, L. and Jaensson (2004), "Small Firm's Internationalization for Development in Tanzania: Exploring the Network Phenomenon", *International Journal of Social Economics*, 159-172.

Ruzzier, M., R.D. Hisrich and B. Antoncic (2006), "SME Internationalization Research: Past, Present and Future", *Journal of Small Business and Enterprise Development*, 476-496.

Sdiri, H. and M Ayadi (2014), "Internationalization and Innovation Profitability: The Case of Tunisian Service Firms", *Problems and Perspectives in Management*, 40-50.

Theocharakis, P.V. (2014), "Challenges of Managing High Technology Ventures", available at: http://www.ltp.ntua.gr/:http://www.ltp.ntua.gr/uploads/lq/j4/lqj4LNcq9533rrQGJxVbsQ/Challenges-1.pdf.

Tiwari, R. and S. Buse (2007), "Barriers to Innovation in SMEs:Can Internationalization Mitigate their Effect?", Proceedings of the First European Conference on Knowledge for Growth: Role and Dynamics of Corporate R&D (CONCORD), Seville.

Vanhaverbeke, P.D. (2012), "Open Innovation in SMEs: How Can Small Companies and Start-ups Benefit from Open Innovation Strategies?".

Ven, A.H. (1986), "Central Problems in the Management of Innovation", *Management Science*, 590-607.

Wickramasekera, R. and S. Mitchell (2009), "Explaining International New Venture Internationalization: Innovation Adoption Model", Australia and New Zealand International Business Academy, Bisbane, Queensland.

Yu, C. and T. Zhang (2010), "Internal Factors Affecting the Organizational Internationalization Process: Evidence From Huawei Case Study", Halmstad, Sweden.

Zen, A. C., M. Amal and W.S. Santos (2014), "Internationalization as an Antecedent of Innovation: An Exploratory Study", *encotron da ANPAD*, 1-3.

Zou, H., X. Liu and P. Ghauri (2010), "Technology Capabilty and the International Stratagies of New Venture", Organizations and Markets in Emerging Economies, 100-119.

8

Financing of Micro Enterprises: Challenges and Prospects

Ramakrushna Panigrahi

Introduction

For a developing economy like India, the importance of the micro, small and medium enterprises (MSMEs) sector cannot be overemphasized, especially when the economy has witnessed rapid growth rates without corresponding increase in employment. Within the MSMEs sector, micro enterprises constitute 81.39 percent of all enterprises and employ bulk of the labour force in India. Together with the entrepreneurial ventures of the SHGs, these very small and micro enterprises have become a source of employment generation and economic activities, specifically in rural India. In fact, India has registered very high growth rates during the last two decades, while many economies have struggled to keep the pace of the economy.

The MSMEs sector has contributed close to 40 percent of the GDP in India and has played a major role in sustenance of such high growth rates in the Indian economy. However, despite such high rates of growth, the critics have termed India's achievement as a phenomenon of 'an era of jobless growth'. To overcome the challenges of rapid employment creation, the focus should be on employment generation at lesser per capita deployment of capital investments, which is possible only in micro and small entrepreneurial ventures. In the present context, the MSMEs sector has assumed significance due to proactive government intervention both at the central and state levels.

The sector has the potential to provide a platform to achieve Millennium Development Goals envisaged by the United Nations. MSMEs have a vital role in dispersal of industries and generation of employment at a much lesser investment requirement. However, the sector faces many challenges such as availability of raw material, lack of entrepreneurial skills, absence of an institutional support system and finally, a formal financial value chain which is conspicuous by its absence.

In fact, the MSMEs sector often faces lack of quality credit facility due to very small size of the business and has never been an avenue of first choice for the formal financial system. Despite the rhetoric and various government schemes to address these issues, availability of formal credit line at low cost, that is suitable to the credit appetite of micro and small entrepreneurs have often been eluding. Apart from access to financial value chain, there are many other challenges for the MSMEs sector to remain relevant and profitable in a fiercely competitive environment. This paper makes an effort to analyze the issues in the financial value chain for the entrepreneurial ventures of SHGS and the micro enterprises from the perspectives of competitiveness and profitability in the contemporary economic environment.

Literature Review on SHGs and Micro Enterprises

The literature on micro finance and MSMEs operations in the context of India has aptly emphasized the rhetoric of social development of the nation. Due to considerable disparity in spatial development, intervention through non-formal financial institutions as a means for income generation through micro enterprises is well appreciated by the policymakers and the development practitioners alike in India. Datta and Raman (2000), in their study, have made an attempt to analyse social cohesion in micro enterprises given the inherent heterogeneity in Indian societies. Similarly, Barbara and Mahanta (2001) have assessed the impact of SHGs-based micro enterprises considering the case of *Gramina Vikash Nidhi*. However, this study does not link per capita economic investments to employment creation in the MSMEs sector. Manimekalai (2001), in her study has made an attempt to analyse the nature and performance of micro enterprises financed through micro finance institutions in Tamil Nadu.

Sivramkrishna and Panigrahi (2001) have provided theoretical economic models on SHGs with a focus on four economic variables. An economic typology of SHGs are well articulated which show that these variables can have a significant effect on micro enterprises' borrowing and demand for credit and push the cost of capital significantly high. The intervention by development agencies like government and other funders can only help kick start a micro enterprise; but sustainability depends on profitability which must be consistent with the cost of funds. The paper throws insights into how the cost of funds plays an important role in sustainability of the micro enterprises.

Madheswaran and Dhramadhikary (2001) find that the success of group lending for micro enterprises are attributable not only to peer monitoring but to other factors such as lending for consumption purposes, including savings among the group.

Yulue and Sahoo (2002) found that most micro enterprises in rural areas are involved in economic activities like rearing goats, poultry, collecting forest products and maintaining livestock for which finances are obtained from MFIs at a very high rate of interest. The study found that awareness among the SHG women on literacy and continuing education, sanitation and health care has increased as compared to their non-SHG peers thereby fulfilling some of the development goals. However, profitability of such micro enterprises launched by SHG members is highly under pressure due to very high cost of funds.

Karnakar and Ghosh (2002) outlined that SHGs provide opportunities for economic empowerment of rural women. They opine that the success stories of a large number of rural women have given a spur to the movement and many banks should link more SHGs as part of their legitimate business activity, thereby accentuating micro enterprises in the rural areas.

Sashtri (2009) has done a comparative study in the context of micro finance and found that such initiatives indeed help in poverty reduction in India, despite many challenges faced by the micro entrepreneurs. Sarumati and Mohan (2011) have analysed the role of micro finance in women empowerment, but the study does not throw much light on economic impact assessment on employment creation and profitability of the micro enterprises.

The study of Pokhriyal and Ghildiyal (2011) documents the role of micro finance institutions in providing financial inclusion to the target population in both rural and urban areas. Though the study suggests raising the amount of loans to stakeholders for better impact, it has not analyzed the potential of employment creation and profitability of the micro enterprises from the cost of funds perspective.

Gundappa (2014) has critically analysed the role of SHGs in the context of empowerment of women. However, impact of SHGs operations on economic well-being is not documented comprehensively in the Indian context. Yadav (2014) has analyzed the significance of micro finance institutions in rural development in India. The analysis of this study focuses on availing credit and increasing women's participation in economic activities through micro enterprises and decision-making.

Chakrabarty (2014) examines the institutional voids and argues to adopt a written code of positive organizational ethics. The study examines whether micro finance institutions serve women borrowers engaged in micro enterprises at the base of the economic pyramid. He argues that a positive organizational ethics code can guide the members towards a higher ethical potential in social contexts that exclude women from market based activities.

Sarmah (2014) has critically analysed the growth of micro finance and micro enterprises linkages through SHGs in India. The study examines the Andhra Pradesh crisis and analyses the growth of Indian micro finance for micro enterprises with MFIs-Bank Linkage programme.

Sharma (2014) has analysed micro finance through SHGs in the context of women empowerment in the state of Sikkim. The study concludes that women empowerment has been achieved due to SHGs operations—enhancing confidence and capacity of women to participate in economic activities through micro enterprises.

Longkumer and Jha (2014) have focused on levels and characteristics of women's empowerment through SHGs. The study finds that political empowerment of women through SHG was very negligible and the reason being the seclusion of women from the political power right from the inception of the society. The study opines that proper measures should be taken by the government so that women can participate in both economic and political fields on equal footing with their male counterparts.

Suprabha (2014) argues that the medium and long-term perspectives of micro finance should be to empower the SHG members to enable them to undertake income generating micro enterprises on a viable and sustainable basis. The study empirically examines the determinants of empowerment of SHGs as micro finance clients to micro enterprise investors. She argues for making micro finance an effective strategic instrument for poverty alleviation through income generating micro enterprise development. She argues that NGOs should play the role of facilitators rather than financers and vertical market integration strategy is required to link micro enterprise products with the markets to ensure better profitability.

Nagaraja (2014) has argued for women empowerment through SHGs. Through a case study of Chitradurga district, he finds that 86 percent of the respondents in the study could solve their personal problems through micro enterprises and 80 percent agreed that they were empowered. He advocates creating conducive environment to give boost to women and empower them through income generation activities.

Manikonda (2014) finds that though access to credit has been seen as a motivational factor behind the formation of SHGs that promote micro enterprises, the potential goes beyond economics and loan management. The study finds that by joining MFIs, women were significantly benefited in all social aspects in a significant manner.

Aruna (2015) has analyzed the problems faced by MSMEs entrepreneurs in Visakhapatnam and found that they mainly face the problems of raw materials, marketing, and under-utilization of capacity and availability of low cost finance.

Ali and Hussain (2014) have articulated the problems of MSMEs in India and found that in most cases, lack of credit from banks pose a major challenge for MSME entrepreneurs to sustain profits in the face of intense competition from multinational companies.

Agwu and Emeti (2014) have outlined the issues and challenges faced by small and medium scale enterprises in Nigeria. The study finds that about 80 percent of the enterprises are stifled because of poor financing and lack of low cost finance for small-scale enterprises.

Chandraiah and Vani (2014) have analyzed the prospects and problems of MSMEs sector in India and found that despite the huge contribution from the sector to manufacturing, access to finance is the most important impediment for the sustainability of the MSME sector.

Most of the studies available in the literature have highlighted the importance of availability of low cost finance for the success of micro enterprises. The studies that focus on SHGs are unanimous on the finding that the sector has great potential to achieve Millennium Development Goals and creating enough income generation activities thereby facilitating generation of employment. However, no study has focused on integration of non-formal financial sector especially MFIs with that of the initiatives of micro enterprises for greater and focused achievements of employment creation and enhanced contribution to GDP.

Despite the initiatives by the government, 90 percent of micro and small enterprises fail due to a lack comprehensive support system that can make them sustainable by ensuring profitability. As of now, from the survey of literature, it is evident that no study has made an attempt to analyze the potential of integration of MFIs and SHGs with the MSMEs sector in a comprehensive manner. This paper makes an attempt to bridge this gap in the existing literature by providing an analytical theoretical framework of a comprehensive ecosystem that can make the MSMEs sector financially sustainable and profitable thereby enhancing its contribution much more significantly in the economy.

Objectives of the Study

The major objectives of the present study are as follows:

1. To analyze the growth and challenges to success of MSMEs sector in India.
2. To analyze the issues and intricacies of accessing low cost finance for the MSMEs sector.
3. To ascertain whether integration of MSMEs sector with the MFIs will make the sector more effective in creating employment and income with a better success rate.

The study is primarily based on secondary sources of data published by the Ministry of MSMEs and other ministries of the Government of India. Most of the statistics reported in the present study has been sourced from these official sources. The study provides an analytical framework for integration of SHGs with micro enterprises for better success of entrepreneurial ventures of micro and very micro firms based on the author's observation of the SHGs sector and micro entrepreneurs and secondary sources of data published by authentic sources.

MSMEs Sector: Challenges to Success in India

The MSMEs sector has grown significantly during the last

decade. The number of enterprises have grown from 1.73 lakh units in the year 2007-08 to 4.25 lakh units during the year 2014-15 (GoI, 2016) registering a double digit compounded annual growth rate over the years. Among the enterprises, micro enterprises constitute 81.39 percent of total MSMEs whereas the medium enterprises are only to the extent of 1.9 percent. During the year 2016, the highest number of registered enterprises was reported from the state of Tamil Nadu, followed by the state of Gujarat.

Despite such growth of the sector, it is observed that a majority of micro enterprises do not remain profitable and cannot survive for more than five years. In India, the failure rate is very high despite all the schemes of the government. The major reasons for failure can be summarized in terms of access to finance, lack of managerial skills especially in the micro enterprises, inadequate basic infrastructure, lack of strategic planning, limited access to marketing network and supply chain, poor technology base, lack of skilled workers and extremely competitive environment in the post-globalization era. Most often, as is evident in the literature, more than 80 percent of the micro enterprises are stifled because of high cost of finance and poor quality of credit line for the business. The micro enterprises lack depth of financial resources to withstand even minor market turbulences unlike big business houses they compete with, making them unsustainable and unprofitable and as a result they find it difficult to compete and survive.

SHGs, MFIs and Entrepreneurial Ventures

Self-help groups (SHGs) in India have grown significantly over the last two decades. From the literature, it is evident that the economics of micro finance and micro enterprises views lack of accessibility to low cost finance in a market framework as the primary reason for the inability of formal banking sector and financial institutions to profitably serve the needs of the micro enterprises.

Typically, the size of micro enterprises comprises of 1-4

personnel and a very low level of capital deployment. Due to its small ticket size, formal FIs never found this sector an attractive avenue to lend their funds. However, in the last 15-16 years in India, various innovative schemes have found ways out of the impasse, offering credit to the poor entrepreneurs engaged in micro enterprises. These schemes have increased the loan recovery rates and reduced the high fixed costs in dealing with small and frequent loans, thereby allowing FIs to give micro entrepreneurs access to credit at a reasonable cost. There are many schemes to promote and facilitate access to low cost finance for micro entrepreneurs in many countries such as Grameen Bank in Bangladesh, the BancoSol in Bolivia, KREEP in Kenya, the National Bank for Agriculture and Rural Development (NABARD) in India and many more such institutions.

In India, the SHGs seek to enhance their corpus fund by obtaining grants and loans from NGOs, Government schemes and FIs, including commercial banks and re-finance organizations like NABARD and Small Industries Development Bank of India (SIDBI). Though SHG credit remains a small fraction of the total refinance to the rural sector in India, it has grown into an important credit delivery system for the rural micro enterprises.

In the year 1999, NABARD envisaged the SHG-Bank Linkage Programme to "cover at least one-third of the rural population by the year 2008 through one million SHGs" and in fact achieved it in doing so. In 2016, at least 7.9 million SHGs, which were involved in micro enterprises and creating employment for the rural India were linked to FIs for credit delivery system. However, despite the extensive network, the cost of borrowing for micro entrepreneurs through SHGs has remained at exceedingly high levels, making them unprofitable and unsustainable.

The following section deals with the problems of micro entrepreneurs and why they often fail in the face of intense competition.

SHGs and Micro Enterprises: Problem of Scalability

Micro enterprises in India constitute the majority of the MSME sector. As reported by the MSMEs Ministry, more than 80 percent of the MSMEs belong to the micro category. It is observed that most of these enterprises may be categorized as entrepreneur-centric enterprises where self-employment is perceived as an end. Only a fraction of micro enterprises employ a few people. If we analyze the SHG sector, we find that most of the SHG operations resemble the modus operandi of micro enterprises where the objective is income generation through self-employment. As discussed earlier, as of 2016, there were close to 8 million operational SHGs which got an active support from NABARD, SIDBI and other formal and informal institutions including the NGOs. Against 8 million SHGs, the number of reported micro enterprises is less than half a million in India. This shows that there is a huge potential to increase the number of micro enterprises through the MSMEs sector by integrating them with SHGs. This will hugely benefit the employment generation objective of India, which has been witnessing jobless growth over the past few years.

However, there are major challenges which are faced by the SHGs. Though their number and success stories are mostly anecdotal and quite impressive, they face a major problem of *scalability*. It is being observed that a member-entrepreneur of the SHGs exhibit exemplary abilities in managing very micro businesses which involve much lesser amount of finances. Despite the fact that most often the cost of funds are exorbitantly high, [1] they are able to run the operation successfully, which is evident from the fact that the loan recovery rates are above 99 percent [2] in the case of SHGs. However, when it comes to scale up their operations with availability of larger funds, the same entrepreneurs are not able to sustain the profitability, even though the cost of larger funds is comparable to the rates of the formal financial sector.

The problem of scalability occurs due to lack of skills of

the entrepreneur to run a larger operation, lack of access to market and absence of a supply chain infrastructure for small and micro players. Also, they cannot enjoy the economies of scale compared to the established enterprises as they cannot enhance the scale to a minimum threshold level to enjoy scale economies. It is observed that when a micro entrepreneur has attempted to scale up the operations [3] with backing of finances, they fail more often than they succeed. This is because of lack of skills of the entrepreneur and absence of a robust financial market and effective supply chain for inputs and output of the micro enterprises.

However, the problem of scalability can be effectively addressed through institutional intervention. As of now, there are many institutions which address the issues of MSMEs and micro entrepreneurs from multitudes of perspectives. For example, the National Skill Development Authority of India has introduced many schemes to promote entrepreneurship. There are 12 ministries of the Government of India which are involved in skill development schemes in various capacities. If there is better cohesion and coordination among the departments, many issues of the scalability problem of micro enterprises can be effectively addressed.

Entrepreneurial Ventures of SHGs versus MSMEs

The SHG-induced enterprises have been quite successful in employment generation and have been economically viable in India without any reported financial delinquency. With very high rates of recovery of close to 99 percent, they are a delight for any lender looking at making good returns on money. It is observed that the high recovery rates are ensured due to peer pressure of the group members, which *per se* is good for the micro enterprises as they refrain from diverting the money from the purported investment avenue.

The entrepreneurial ventures of the SHGs have become most sought after avenues for deployment of funds by the lenders of both formal and the informal sector. Micro enterprises of the MSMEs sector on the other hand have great potential for employment generation and can contribute to GDP substantially provided they become financially viable. However, it is observed that a majority of these ventures fail due to a variety of reasons including access to low cost credit and financial prudence being the most prominent one. As a result, both the formal and informal lenders of funds usually take a defensive approach fearing bad loans making it not a very favourite avenue, despite the institutional support and government intervention. While entrepreneurial ventures of SHGs are quite successful financially, most often the micro enterprises fail despite having a similar operational framework. If there is synergy between these two sectors, the purpose of the MSMEs sector can be better achieved and the various issues of development goals can be successfully met.

Conclusion

The MSMEs sectors, specifically the micro enterprises share many operational features with the modus operandi of the entrepreneurial ventures of the SHGs sector. While the entrepreneurial ventures of the SHG sector have become quite successful in terms of financial viability, the MSMEs sector fails most often due to lack of financial prudence along with many other bottlenecks. Micro enterprises can learn from the experiences of the entrepreneurial ventures of the SHGs. The MSMEs Ministry needs to support the MSMEs sector by providing access to formal markets and supply chain logistics to make the sector more successful and sustainable.

It may be noted that, proactive intervention by the MSMEs sector is required to impart necessary skills to run the enterprises, as the observed skill gaps are too wide in India. There is a need for better cohesion among all the agencies to intervene in the MSMEs sector to bring down the failure rates of the ventures. If the project is well-planned with financial prudence as exhibited by the ventures of the SHGs and accountability for financial viability is fixed along with logistical support, MSMEs sector will have a much larger potential to create employment and income and contribute more significantly to the GDP of India while achieving the development goals.

Endnotes

1. It is observed that a typical interest rate varies between 24 percent and 36 percent per annum against a prime lending rate of around 11 percent in the Indian economy.
2. It is evident from many studies that the recovery rates are above 99 percent. The interaction of the author with SHGs groups in the state of Karnataka, Tamil Nadu and Odisha confirm the high recovery rates despite the fact that the members have the obligations of a very high rate of servicing the loan.
3. Many of the SHGs entrepreneur run micro enterprises in a rural or a semi-urban set up. For example, typically their operations include tea shops, small stores, goat rearing, tailoring etc. As one can observe, in a typical village set up, the demand is highly restricted. The same village cannot support multiple tea shops, multiple tailors and any such venture. In the case of goat rearing, an entrepreneur can rear up to a limited number of goats which can be sold locally. When they try to rear in larger numbers, lack of integration with the supply chain and logistics play a major hindrance, forcing the entrepreneurs to go for distress selling at a loss. For any such enterprise looking forward to scale up operations, lack of accessibility to formal markets would result in a micro enterprise sustaining losses which was otherwise making a profit when the level of output was less.

References

Barbara, S. and R. Mahanta (2001), "Microfinance through Self-Help Groups and its Impact: A Case of Rashtriya Gramina Vikash Nidhi Credit and Savings Program in Assam", *Indian Journal of Agricultural Economics*, Vol. 56, No. 3.

Aruna, N. (2015), "Problems Faced by Micro, Small and Medium Enterprises: A Special Reference to Small Entrepreneurs in Visakhapatanam", *IOSR Journal of Business and Management*, Vol. 17, No. 4, 43-49.

Ali, Anis and Firoz Husain (2014), "MSMEs in India: Problems, Solutions and Prospects in Present Scenario", *International*

Journal of Engineering and Management Sciences, Vol. 5. No. 2, 109-115.

Agwu, Mba Okechukwu and Cletus Izunwanne Emeti (2014), "Issues, Challenges and Prospects of Small and Medium Scale Enterprises (SMEs) in Port-Hacourt City, Nigeria", *European Journal of Sustainable Development*, Vol. 3, No. 1, 101-114.

Chakrabarty, Subrata (2014), "Institutionalizing ethics in institutional Voids: Building Positive Ethical Strength to Serve Women Microfinance Borrowers in Negative Contexts", *Journal of Business Ethics*, Vol. 119, No. 4.

Chandraiah, M. and R. Vani (2014), "The Prospects and Problems of MSMEs Sector in India: An Analytical Study", *International Journal of Business and Management Intervention*, Vol. 3, No. 8, 27-40.

Datta, S.K. and A. Raman (2000), "Can Heterogeneity and Social Cohesion Exist in Self-help Groups: Evidence from Group Lending in AP in India", *Indian Journal of Agricultural Economics*, Vol. 33, No. 4.

Fernandez, A. (1998), "The MYRADA Experience: Alternative Management Systems for Savings and Credit of the Rural Poor", second edition, MYRADA: Bangalore.

Government of India (2016), "Annual Report 2015-16", Ministry of Micro Small and Medium Enterprises, New Delhi, available at: http://msme.gov.in/WriteReadData/DocumentFile/MEME%20ANNUAL%20REPORT%202015-16%20ENG.pdf.

Gundappa, Mudakappa (2014), "Microfinance and Empowerment of Women: An Impact Study of SHGs", *Indian Streams Research Journal*, Vol. 4, No. 8.

Karnakar and Ghosh (2002), "Economic Empowerment of Rural Women through SHGs", *Economic and Political Weekly*, Vol. 4, 24-25.

Longkumer, M. and K.K. Jha (2014), "Women's Empowerment through SHGs: Characteristics and Levels", *International Journal of Social Relevance and Concern*, Vol. 2, No. 2, February.

Madheswaran, S. and Amita Dharmadhikary (2001), "Empowering Rural Women through Self-help Groups: Lessons from Maharashtra Rural Credit Project", *Indian Journal of Agricultural Economics*, Vol. 56, No. 3.

Manikonda, Rajani (2014), "Benefits through SHGs: Perception of

Women in Andhra Pradesh", *European Academic Research*, Vol. 2, No. 7, October.

Manimekalai, N. Rajeswari (2001), "Nature and Performance of informal Self Help Groups: A Case from Tamil Nadu", *Indian Journal of Agricultural Economics*, Vol. 56, No. 3.

Nagaraja, G. (2014), "Women Empowerment through Women Self-Help Groups: A Case Study of Chitradurga District", *International Journal of Multidisciplinary Advanced Experimental Research*, Vol. 1, No. 1.

NABARD (2014), "Status of Microfinance in India, 2012-13", NABARD, Mumbai.

Pokhriyal, A.K. and V. Ghildiyal (2011), "Progress of Microfinance and Financial Inclusion: A Critical Analysis of SHG-Bank Linkage Program in India", *International Journal of Economics and Finance*, Vol. 3, No. 2, May.

Sarmah, Gunindra Nath (2014), "Growth of Microfinance and SHGs Linkage in India: A Critical Analysis", *Zenith International Journal of Business Economics and Management Research*, Vol. 4, No. 12.

Sarumati, S. and K. Mohan (2011), "Role of Microfinance in Women's Empowerment: An Empirical Study in Pondicherry Region Rural SHGs", *Journal of Management and Science*, Vol. 1, No. 1.

Sashtri, Rajesh Kumar (2009), "Microfinance and Poverty Reduction in India: A Comparative Study in Asian Countries", *African Journal of Business Management,* Vol. 3, No. 4.

Sharma, Gopal (2014), "Microfinance through SHGs and the Empowerment of Women: A Case Study of Some Selected SHGs of Sikkim", *Asian Journal of Multidisciplinary Studies*, Vol. 2, No. 7.

Sivramkrishna, Sashi and R. Panigrahi (2001), "An Economic Model of Self-help Groups: Policy Implications for Banks and NGO Initiatives", *Journal of International Development*, Vol. 13, 1119-1130.

Suprabha, K.R. (2014), "Empowerment of Self-help Groups Towards Micro Enterprise Development", *Economics and Finance*, Elsevier, Vol. 11, 410-422.

Yadav, Rajesh K. (2014), "Significance of Microfinance Institutions in Rural Development of India", *International Letters of Social and Humanistic Sciences*, Vol. 10, No. 2.

Yulue and Sahoo (2002), "A Study on SHG and Tribal Women Empowerment in Maharashtra", *Economic and Political Weekly*, Vol. 4, 14-18.

9

Burden of Risk-based Pricing by Financing Banks on SMEs

B.P. Mishra

Introduction

The financing of SMEs has attracted much attention in recent years and there is a perception among academic and policy makers that SMEs lack appropriate financing and hence, need to receive special assistance. Banks are the single largest provider of external finance to SMEs, but the ways in which financial institutions operate in new regulatory norms is biased against SME financing and are at the root of inadequate financing of SMEs.

While the promoters of SMEs have limited muscle to raise fresh equity, borrowing from banks has never been easy either. Research across space has established that SMEs face formidable hurdles in order to access credit, especially institutional credit. The factors that restrict credit flows to the sector include information opacity, inadequate collateral, insufficient legal status, a high level of transaction costs and their inability to cope with complexities of dealing with formal financial institutions. Notwithstanding the increase in credit outstanding to the sector over the years, access to adequate and timely credit at a reasonable cost is a critical problem faced by SMEs in India.

Financing of SMEs has again attracted the attention of many commercial banks who have found a profitable business proposition in them. Traditionally, financing SMEs has been fought with greater risk due to small size of the loan, large number of loan accounts (difficult to monitor), lack of adequate and systematic information base, inadequate credit standing, collateral and absence of any credible repayment track record etc. In the above background, accessing the credit worthiness of the SMEs has been really a challenge for the commercial banks. While the risk-based pricing by the formal financial setup has never been a solution and consequently never accepted by the business community, the rating of the SMEs has proved to be a boon for the banks. The rating of SMEs is more of a risk assessment measure rather than a pricing tool. It has a direct impact on the quality of the loan portfolio of commercial banks, resulting in increased capital requirements.

Further, Basel II requirements outline that risk perception of individual assets of the banks will determine the capital to be allocated against that particular asset. Hence, risk profile of assets is now more of a capital adequacy requirement. Hence, banks need to rate borrower/company as a whole than individual facilities hither to. To make the matter worse for SMEs, the Reserve Bank of India has floated a draft report of the Working Group on Pricing of Credit in April 2014 which primarily asks banks to price credit, among other factors, inclusive of credit risk premium and tenor premium.

Indian banks have been using internal systems to assess the credit worthiness of their borrowers. Under internal rating based (IRB) approach, it will be up to the banks to characterize the risk factor of the borrowers and loans in their portfolio by means of a limited number of risk categories or rating classes. Inconsistencies in rating may become a source of adverse selection and new business risk for banks. While booking SME business, all public sector banks (PSBs) have used different rating methodology, but the parameters used can be broadly classified as hard facts (objective) and soft parameters (subjective), as a scoring model to arrive at the final rating. The parameters include financials, management quality, business risk, account behaviour (in case of existing accounts), and regulatory compliance etc.

In response to RBI's initiative, different credit risk assessment (CRA) models in evaluating a borrower customer, have emerged which is at present purely internal to respective banks and not a part of the public domain. Thus, the risk perception of a company/unit by different banks may be varied, though a major emphasis is put on the historical data i.e. past years' balance sheets and future projections submitted by the borrower company. It is still relatively little known about actual functioning and consistency of bank's internal ratings and implied ex-ante risk in bank loan portfolios. It opens up a wide area of research to examine individual bank's modus operandi in integrating ground level risk appreciation and capturing them in risk assessment exercise which affects portfolio risk dimension of the whole bank in an aggregated manner.

The present study covers SMEs in Odisha, (an Eastern Indian state) which are not listed and are mostly small in size, and more susceptible to external shocks, seasonality, technology obsolescence etc. For these SMEs, profit is a major criterion in order to have a long-term viability. Hence, bankers run the risk of holding on to a relatively riskier portfolio to be monitored on a continuous basis with almost no option to exit if warranted. In the light of above, the existing rating tools used by PSBs are to be effective in assessing borrowers and these should have the capabilities to support SME growth in the state. The study aims to test whether existing rating tools are actually capturing the risk potential of SMEs, when employed by the operating staff at the ground level.

The remainder of this paper proceeds with different sections offering literature review, outlining the data set details and methodology employed, followed by illustrative analysis, results obtained and a few concluding remarks.

Literature Review

To what extent a different treatment of retail credit and SME loans is justified will depend on at least two factors: the ability of banks' internal risk rating systems to adequately capture the differences between different loans and different types of assets, and the methods used to calculate the relevant risk measure. Several authors have studied the ability of banks' internal ratings systems to handle differences between (portfolios of) assets and the implications for credit risk measurement and the eventual functioning of Basel II.

Gordy (2000) shows that ratings-based bucket models of credit can be reconciled with the general class of credit Value-at-Risk (VaR) models.

Carey (2000) concludes that the success of the IRB approach will depend on the extent to which it will take into account differences in assets and portfolio characteristics, such as granularity, risk properties and remaining maturities.

Jacobson et al. (2002) found that IRB parameters such as the target forecasting horizon, the method to estimate average probabilities of default (PDs) and banks' business cycle sensitivity will also affect the way in which the IRB system can function.

Carey and Hrycay (2001) study the effect of internal risk rating systems on estimated portfolio credit risk and find that some of the commonly used methods to estimate average probabilities of default (PDs) by rating class are potentially subject to bias, instability, and gaming.

Jacobson et al. (2005) investigated the consistency of internal ratings at two major Swedish banks. They found that loan size and portfolio size are very important determinants of the shape of credit loss distributions and that the banks differ significantly in their perceptions of an identical loan portfolio's riskiness.

Dietsch and Petey (2004) also find that SMEs are riskier than large businesses and that PDs and asset correlations are not negative, as assumed by Basel II, but positively related to each other. [1]

Glennon and Nigro (2003) analyze small business repayment behaviour on small business administration loans and determine that default characteristics can vary widely within the SME segment, depending on the original maturity of the loan.

Data Set and Period

However, SMEs in Odisha rooted more in traditional handicrafts and basic agro-processing, elevated gradually to manufacturing of a span of industrial intermediaries, chemicals and metal-based processing and fabrication etc. The present scenario reflects a robust growth both supported by favourable Government initiatives, export-led growth in mineral sector, and coming in of a large number of outside established corporates in search of green field projects. Hence, the role of SMEs, in coming days, will be very crucial in sustaining the ongoing process of integration of the state with national mainstream.

The banks in general, are active participants in supporting SMEs in the state with their principle role of being a purveyor of credit. Credit dispensation apart, a bank's role as a friend, philosopher and guide to the new entrepreneur class is highly commendable. At the forefront, the public sector banks led by State Bank of India (SBI) have seen to it that SMEs do not suffer from necessary financial support and ensured continued expansion of SMEs by providing asset-based finance cemented through relationship lending technology.

The empirical study covered the period between 2004 (April) and 2008 (March) which represents a boom cycle marked by significant growth in the economy both at the national level as also at the state level. As regards the state of the economy during that period, at an all-India level, macroeconomic fundamentals continued to inspire confidence and the investment climate was full of optimism. There was no doubt that the economy has moved to a higher growth plane, with growth of GDP at market prices exceeding 8 percent every year since 2003-04. [2] Odisha's economy had been following a high growth trajectory in those years. During the relevant period, keeping with state GDP growth, all banks in

Odisha increased their lending to SME sector so that fund availability was never a constraint. From all perspectives, when the economy is buoyant and the risk perception is low (in general) and the financial performance of borrower units are off-beat, the banks would have found the risk assessment of borrower units up to their expectation before expanding in to new exposure or deepening the existing exposure level.

Sample Bank Data

Further analysis of banks' exposure to SMEs by the public sector banks in Odisha, reveals that there are only 10-12 banks who have major contribution to the total pool. As proportion to the total SME credit outstanding by PSBs in Odisha during the relevant period and in subsequent years, SBI had a major and dominant share in the total basket. In view of the dominant role of SBI and its continued active role in promoting SMEs in Odisha for past five decades, the samples were chosen from the borrower's profile of SBI spread over parts of Odisha operating during the relevant period between 2004-05 and 2007-2008.

Data Collection

The study is based on primary data. The data was collected from customers, their financial consultants and from the credit officials handling those accounts at respective branches or credit appraisal centres of the bank. It was difficult to collect the rating grade calculation sheet from bank records.

The data set has a lot of granularities as regards facilitating the analysis. Financial information of the unit in all years from 2004-05 to 2007-08 like net sales, operating profit, PBT, PBT/set sales, PAT, cash accrual, PBDIT, PUC, TNW, TOL/TNW, total current assets, NWC, rating awarded by the bank, unit specific data regarding enterprise legal status (composition), category industry, activity and limit enjoyed from the Bank etc. was captured. Total data was collected for approximately 150 samples and ultimately analyzed for 90 samples as they have consistent and continuous information relevant to the analysis. This study uses a stratified random sampling procedure to make sure that samples have proportional representation of population sub-groups.

Research Methodology

This is an analytical study and hence a system of procedures and techniques of analysis was applied to quantitative data. The study aims at specifying and interpreting relationships. The analysis was done at two levels. First, as already stated, the rating exercise was done on the basis of quantitative and qualitative parameters giving weightage in different proportions by different banks, for assigning a rating to any enterprise. While the individual component of quantitative parameter is captured in the data, the qualitative parameter is taken as a residual from the aggregate value for total scoring. We have used a multi-variant regression analysis to establish a relationship between quantitative and qualitative factors in explaining the rating assigned by the bank to the enterprises over a period of four years.

The modes of Least Squares Regression equations are –

Y = rating
C = constant
Variable 1 = current ratio
Variable 2 = PBDIT interest
Variable 3 = PBT/net sales
Variable 4 = ROCE
Variable 5 = TOL/TNW
Variable 6 = trend
Variable 7 = inventory/net sales + receivable gross sales
(No. of days) [constant variable]
Variable-8 = qualitative factors

$Y = \alpha + \beta_1 V_1 + \beta_2 V_2 + \beta_3 V_3 + \beta_4 V_4 + \beta_5 V_5 + \beta_6 V_6 + \beta_7 V_7 + u$ (Regression-1)

$Y = \alpha + \beta_1 V_1 + \beta_2 V_2 + \beta_3 V_3 + \beta_4 V_4 + \beta_5 V_5 + \beta_6 V_6 + \beta_7 V_7 + \beta_8 V_8 + u$ (Regression-2)

We have made regression analysis in two stages. In the first stage, the regression does not include the qualitative factors and in the second one, it does include the same.

Regression Result

As a first step of analysis, in both the regression results, it is observed that the coefficients are negative implying that each of the independent variable had a negative effect on the dependent variable (Table 9.1).

This implies that any dependent variable increase i.e., say increase in the value of current asset will decrease the value of rating (Y). This is implicit in the model itself.

When we state that CA ratio increases by one unit, it increases the aggregate scoring, say changing the rating grade from 3 to 2 which is an improvement in the assigned rating to the unit. In case of TOL/TNW parameter, the point awarded is in a decreasing order to actual ratio, the higher the ratio, the lower the points. Hence, a unit change will directly affect the final rating decision.

The regression carried out in this study reveals the impact of various financial parameter rankings on the overall rating of the units of the bank. Two regression models are executed: one with all the possible financial parameter rankings and time trend, and the other with not only financial parameter rankings but also a composite factor comprising the rankings of all the qualitative factors along with time trend.

The first regression results reveal that the ranking of all financial ratio indicators explain only about 8 percent variation of the total ranking (see R^2 value).

Except the time trend, as expected, the rankings of all the ratio indicators are though mostly found negatively influencing the overall ranking; their influences are, however, surprisingly quite insignificant. This result explains the need for the examination of possible presence of other qualitative factors to see if they jointly explain the overall ranking behaviour of the bank ratings.

Table 9.1: Dependent Variable: RATING, Method: Least Squares, Sample: 360, Included observation: 360

Regression: I

Variable	Coefficient	Std. Error	t-Statistic	Prob.
Variable 7	3.022389	0.180167	16.77548	0.0000
Variable 1	-0.064178	0.037955	-1.690913	0.0917
Variable 2	0.008506	0.039996	0.212670	0.8317
Variable 3	-0.028114	0.024282	-1.157830	0.2477
Variable 4	-0.036356	0.040398	-0.899943	0.3688
Variable 5	-0.041702	0.036450	-1.144098	0.2534
Variable 6	0.212575	0.045951	4.626159	0.0000
R-squared	0.080336	Mean dependent var		2.858333
adjusted R-squared	0.064705	S.D. dependent var		1.286067
S.E. of regression	1.243764	Akaike info criterion		3.293415
Sum squared resid	546.0734	Schwarz criterion		3.368978
Log likelihood	-585.8147	Hannan-Quinn criter.		3.323461
F-statistic	5.139321	Durbin-Watson stat		0.811625
Prob. (F-statistic)	0.000044			

Regression-II

Variable	Coefficient	Std. Error	t-Statistic	Prob.
Variable 7	3.635879	0.029191	124.5540	0.0000
Variable 1	-0.068248	0.006049	-11.28333	0.0000
Variable 2	-0.071121	0.006410	-11.09477	0.0000
Variable 3	-0.084355	0.003900	-21.63151	0.0000
Variable 4	-0.098629	0.006460	-15.26758	0.0000
Variable 5	-0.088499	0.005823	-15.19922	0.0000
Variable 6	-0.098874	0.007796	-12.68221	0.0000
Variable 8	-0.084318	0.000724	-116.3961	0.0000
R-squared	0.976711	Mean dependent var		2.858333
Adjusted R-squared	0.976248	S.D. dependent var		1.286067
S.E. of regression	0.198206	Akaike info criterion		-0.377045
Sum squared resid	13.82857	Schwarz criterion		-0.290688
Log likelihood	75.86818	Hannan-Quinn criter.		-0.342708
F-statistic	2108.896	Durbin-Watson stat		1.534909
Prob. (F-statistic)	0.000000			

Our second regression model therefore considers both quantitative ratio indicators and a composite quality indicator comprising all the qualitative factors, in addition to time trend to explain their influences on the overall ranking. The results show that the presence of both quantitative and qualitative factors jointly explains around 97 percent (see R^2 value) of the total variation of the overall rank. The addition of one composite qualitative factor not only enormously increases the total variation by 90 percent but also enhances drastically the influences of individual financial ratio indicators.

On a closer look at the coefficients of both qualitative and quantitative indicators, their individual influences that enhance the overall rank remain within 7-9 percent.

The finding that the trend variable in the first regression model appears to be the only variable enhancing the overall rank behaviour by 21 percent does not seem satisfactory. It is precisely because the same variable is found to have deteriorated the overall rank by 10 percent. Therefore, our results indicate that the omission of relevant factors in any model exhibit conflicting signals concerning the possible impact of individual ratio indicators.

Limitation of the Analysis

The sample size is a limiting factor. The static financial data on inventory/net sale + receivable/gross sales (days) was not available on a continuous and consistent basis in the sample data. Hence, we have taken it as a constant in the regression analysis.

Conclusion

In the context of the analysis of the results, it can be safely concluded that the existing rating tools used by the banks in Odisha (that include all public sector banks) having the same rating methodology are not able to capture the true risk profile of borrowers they are usually serving. The model at the macro level being selected to assign and capture risk of the borrower, at ground level is fairly and squarely getting distorted. The operational entities, to book business and to grow, are indulging in adverse selection. As a result, the risk profile of the aggregate level is not a true reflection of the aggregate risk of individual loans in the portfolio. As a result, the estimation of PD, LGD and EAD are not correctly estimated by banks. This study shows that: subjective judgments are indeed capable of yielding valuable information and improve credit rating systems which are based solely on quantitative information by considerable amount.

1. Default risk is most likely not homogenous within internal rating classes. Banks, in our study, have not implemented internal borrower risk-rating systems in such a way that they result in consistent estimates of portfolio credit losses.
2. Internal credit rating system have varied level of functions such as guiding loan origination process, portfolio monitoring, analysis of adequacy of loan provision, profitability analysis, loan pricing, risk capital allocation, etc. In India, ratings are rarely being used to price the loan and in some cases profitability analysis of customer.
3. With a bundle score, loan origination is determined on the basis of allotted rating. Linking pricing to rating put a special stress on the rating system to retain a customer in the portfolio, when the competition is too high.
4. Introduction of risk based pricing by banks will put the SMEs in further worsening their finance delivery as their current rating in most of the cases are inflated.

A CRISIL study on the financial performance of over 3,000 rated SMEs reveals that every percentage point increase in interest rate would lead to a decline of 1.40 percent, on an average, in SMEs profits (Business Standard, February, 2011). Credit literature states that lower level of business activity force small firms to access credit market and SMEs are also sensitive about the price of the credit. Thus, linking pricing of credit to the credit risk and tenor premium will be the "last nail in the coffin", especially for, smaller of the SMEs pack.

Endnotes

1. The consultative document that the Basel Committee released in 2003. The final text contains a number of modifications. In addition to the introduction of expected and unexpected losses, these concern mainly minor changes in the calibration of the risk weight mappings, e.g., the assumed values of the correlations for SME loans and retail credit.

2. Economic Survey, 2007-08 Government of India, "State of the Economy", Oxford, New Delhi.

References

Acs, Zoltan J. and David. B. Audretsh, (1990), "Innovations in Small Firms", Cambridge, MA: MIT Press.

Allen, L., G. DeLong and A. Saunders (2003), "Issues in the Credit Risk Modelling of Retail Markets", available at: www.defaultrisk.com.

Altman, E.I. and G. Sabato (2005), "Modelling Credit Risk for SMEs: Evidence from the US market", available at: www.ssrn.com.

Altman, E.I. and Anthony Saunders (1977), "An Analysis and Critique of the BIS Proposal on Capital Adequacy and Rating", *Journal of Banking and Finance*, 1(1), 29-54.

Ayyagiri, M., T. Beck and A. Demirguc-Kunt (2007), "Small and Medium Enterprises across the Globe", *Small Business Economics,* 29, 415-434.

Basel Committee on Banking Supervision (2001, 2003, 2004 and 2006), "International Convergence of Capital Measurement and Capital Standards", available at: www.bis.org.

Beck, T. et al. (2006), "Small and Medium Size Enterprises: Access to Finance as a Growth Constraint", *Journal of Banking and Finance*, 30, 2931-2943.

Beck, T. et al. (2009), "Banking SME around the World: Lending Practices, Business Models, Drivers and Obstacles", World Bank Policy Research Working Paper 4785.

Berger, A.N. and N.K. Black (2008), "Bank Size, Lending Technologies and Small Business Finance", Working Paper, University of California.

Bhatia, Mohan (2006), "Credit Risk Management and Basel II: An Implementation Guide", Risk Books, London.

Das, Kesab (ed.) (2011), "Micro and Small Enterprises in India: The Era of Reforms", New Delhi: Routledge India.

Dietsch, M. and J. Petey (2000), "The Credit Risk in SME Loans Portfolio: Modelling Issues, Pricing and Capital Requirements", *Journal of Banking and Finance,* 26, 303-322.

"Economic Survey Odisha, 2010-11", Government of Odisha, Oxford University Press: New Delhi.

Government of India (GoI) (2004), "Final Results: Third All India Census of Small Scale Industries, 2001-2002", New Delhi, Ministry of Industry.

Alan Hughes and A. Cosh A. (1994), "Size, Financial Structure and Profitability", in Hughes and Storey (eds.), 'Financing Small Firms', London, Routledge, 64-111.

IFC (2007), "Benchmarking SME Banking Practices in OECD and Emerging Markets".

Levitsky, J. (1986), "World Bank Lending to Small Enterprises: A Review", *Industry and Finance Series*, Vol. 16, The World Bank.

M, Jayadev (2006), "Internal Credit Rating Practices of Indian Banks", *Economic and Political Weekly*, March 18.

Manna, Indrani (2010), "Trends in Select Micro and Small Scale Production Items during Phases of Industrial Slowdown", RBI Working Papers, June 4.

Meera, Sharma (2008), "Management of Financial Institutions with Emphasis on Bank and Risk Management", New Delhi: Prentice-Hall of India.

Miller, M. (ed.) (2003), "Credit Reporting Systems and the International Economy", MIT Press, Cambridge.

Mohan, Rakesh (2002), "Small Scale Industry Policy in India: A Critical Evaluation", in Anne O. Kruger (ed.), 'Economic Policy Reforms and the Indian Economy', New Delhi: Oxford University Press.

Morris, Sebastian, Rakesh Basant, Keshab Dash, K. Ramachandran and Abraham Koshy (2001), "The Growth and Transformation of Small Firms in India", New Delhi: Oxford University Press.

Mustafa Kemal Yilmaz and Ali Kucukcolak (2007), "Effects of Basel II Standards on Small-Medium Size Enterprises: Evidence from the Istanbul Stock Exchange", Marmara University, School of Banking and Insurance.

Roy, Bibek Deb and Laveesh Bhandari (ed.) (2005), "Small Scale Industry in India: Large Scale Exit Problems", New Delhi: Academic Foundation.

Stigliz, J.E. and A. Weiss (1981), "Credit Rationing in Markets with Imperfect Information", *American Economic Review*, 71(3), 912-927.

Stigliz, J.E. and A. Weiss (1985), "Credit Rationing and Collateral", Bell communications Research Economics, Discussion Paper

No. 12.

Tendulkar, S.D. and T.A. Bhavani (1997), "Policy on Modern Small Scale Industries: A Case of Government Failure", *Indian Economic Review*, 32(10), 39-64.

Tor, Jacobson, Jesper Linde and Kasper Roszbach (2005), "Credit Risk versus Capital Requirements under Basel II: Are SME Loans and Retail Credit Really Different", *Riksbank Economic Review*.

Torre, A and S.L. Schmukler (2010), "Bank Involvement with SMEs: Beyond Relationship Lending", *Journal of Banking and Finance*, 34, 2280-2293.

10

Progress and Prospects of MSMEs in Tamil Nadu

L. Ganesan and R. Senthamizh Veena

Introduction

All over the world, micro small and medium enterprises (MSMEs) act as an effective means of development in an economy. These MSMEs have considerable impact on various aspects of an economy like employment generation, reducing poverty, minimising regional imbalance, increasing industrial progress and expanding exports as well. The major advantage of this sector is its low investment with high employment potential of skilled and unskilled persons. The labour intensity of this sector is also comparatively higher than the capital intensive industries. This is a boon for a country like India, which is flooded with enormous human resources (Das, 2014; Katyal and Xaviour, 2015).

In India, the primary responsibility of promotion and development of MSMEs is of the State governments. The Central Government supplements the efforts of the State governments through various initiatives and assist the States in their efforts to encourage entrepreneurship and livelihood opportunities and enhance the competitiveness of MSMEs in the changing economic scenario (MSMED Policy Note, 2016-17). Against this background, it is important to study the various issues of MSMEs in the country. Accordingly, the present study aims to study the progress and prospects of MSMEs in India and specifically in the state of Tamil Nadu.

Literature Review

Katyal and Besty in their paper have discussed about the

issues related to human resources in MSMEs in India. After analysing the contribution of MSMEs to the Indian economy, the researchers have focussed on the HR operations and the minimalist approach mandate systems an MSME should have. They have suggested that, irrespective of the size of the business, every business operations should have a clear talent philosophy guiding vital talent management processes - like talent acquisition, assessment, development, retention and leadership.

S.K. Das in his paper examined the performance of MSMEs in promoting socio-economic development of poor in the state of Odisha. The author claims that the growth of MSMEs is a healthy sign of progress and prosperity in the state of Odisha. Further, the author implies that inherent to the location and natural resources, the state has tremendous potentialities to create ample opportunities in small businesses in various sectors and asserts that entrepreneurship development is a key factor to fight against unemployment, poverty and achieve overall socio-economic growth in the state.

A study of International Finance Corporation (IFC) provides an assessment of the finance for MSMEs in India. It states that the lack of adequate and timely access to finance is the biggest challenge the sector faces. The study also indicates that the financial institutions in the country have limited their exposure to the sector due to a higher risk perception and limited access of MSMEs to immovable collateral. Overall, it suggests that a comprehensive fiscal support, a strong policy framework, and incentives by financial institutions to promote innovation can significantly increase the penetration of formal financial services to the MSME sector.

Objectives and Methodology

The main objective of the study is to analyse the performance of MSMEs in promoting the socio-economic status of Tamil Nadu. The specific objectives of this study are:

1. To analyse the progress of MSMEs in Tamil Nadu.

2. To examine the role and performance of Government policies for MSMEs in Tamil Nadu.
3. To understand the problems of MSMEs in Tamil Nadu.

The present study is entirely based on secondary data collected from various Government publications like Annual Report of the Ministry of Micro, Small and Medium Enterprises of Government of India, Tamil Nadu State Industrial Profile and MSMED Policy Note of Government of Tamil Nadu. The researchers have used simple statistical tools like average, growth rate and percentage to analyse the progress of MSMEs in terms of the number of registered units, investment, production and employment in Tamil Nadu.

Progress of MSMEs in Tamil Nadu:

The state of Tamil Nadu has always been at the forefront of economic growth in the country and also has been among the most industrialised states with a much diversified industrial base. It is ranked among the top three states in the country in terms of industrial output, value addition, number of factories and total workforce in the factories (State Industrial Profile, 2014-15).

Table 10.1 indicates the growth of micro small and medium enterprises after the implementation of MSMED Act, 2006 in terms of number of registered units, level of investment, production and employment in Tamil Nadu.

Number of Registered Units in the State: Table 10.1 shows the growth of the number of registered units in the state. There has been a continuous growth in the number of registered units in the state during 2007-08 to 2014-15 but ended with a negative growth in 2015-16. The number of registered units which was 27,209 in 2007-08 increased significantly to 1,42,136 units in 2015-16. The annual growth rate ranges between 17.78 percent and 39.64 percent during this period, which is a notable achievement. This was made possible mainly due to the business friendly policies and proactive initiatives of the state.

Table 10.1: Progress of MSMEs in Tamil Nadu

Year	Number of Registered Units	Investment (₹ in crore)	Production (₹ in crore)	Employment (Numbers)
2007-08	27209	2547.14	8739.95	242855
2008-09	32049 (17.78)	3557.89 (39.68)	13354.86 (52.80)	294255 (21.16)
2009-10	41799 (30.42)	3214.22 (-9.65)	10880.01 (-18.53)	151743 (-48.43)
2010-11	57902 (38.52)	5872.37 (82.69)	12500.86 (14.89)	405233 (167.05)
2011-12	70758 (22.20)	7429.59 (26.51)	15496.00 (23.95)	502381 (23.97)
2012-13	83348 (17.79)	8751.54 (17.79)	17503.08 (12.95)	583436 (16.13)
2013-14	116393 (39.64)	18939.87 (116.41)	16832.25 (-3.83)	494990 (-15.15)
2014-15	143104 (22.94)	24349.65 (28.56)	59789.70 (255.20)	651180 (31.55)
2015-16 (up to 21.1.2016)	142136 (-0.67)	34411.90 (41.32)	59332.19 (-0.76)	815315 (25.20)
CAGR	22.96	38.46	27.05	16.34

Note: Figures shown in parentheses denotes annual growth rate over the previous year.
Source: MSMED Policy Note, 2016-17, Government of Tamil Nadu.

Investment in MSMEs: From Table 10.1, it can be clearly seen that investment has shown a positive trend throughout the study period, except during 2009-10 which registered a (-) 9.66 percent growth rate. But due to the retrieving efforts of the state, there was massive 82.7 percent growth rate in the following year. Overall, there has been a phenomenal increase in investment from ₹ 2547.14 crore in 2007-08 to ₹ 34,411.90 crore in 2015-16. This remarkable achievement must be credited to the favourable business climate in the state which makes it a safe haven for the investors (State Industrial Profile, 2014-15).

Production of MSMEs: Table 10.1 also reveals the progress of production by MSMEs during 2007-08 to 2015-16 in Tamil Nadu. The value of production has increased substantially from ₹ 8,739.95 crore in 2007-08 to ₹ 59,332.19

crore in 2015-16 with a 27.05 percent CAGR. The annual growth rate of the production shows fluctuating trend with negative growth in 2009-10, 2013-14 and in 2015-16 which is a matter of concern.

Employment in MSMEs: In a labour surplus economy like India, the need for policies and programmes to promote employment generation is of paramount importance. The MSME sector contributes remarkably in providing employment opportunities in the country and specifically in Tamil Nadu.

Table 10.1 depicts the data of employment growth in MSME sector in Tamil Nadu. There has been a continuous growth in the level of employment during 2007-08 to 2015-16, except in 2009-10 and 2013-14. The number of workforce which was 2,94,255 in 2008-09 reduced to 1,51,743 in 2009-10 which was a (-) 48.43 percent decline, but it increased to 4,05,233 in 2010-11. However, no specific reason was reported by the Government for this huge fall in employment in 2009-10. Overall, the number of employment has increased from 2,42,855 in 2007-08 to 8,15,315 in 2015-16 which makes the sector as the second largest provider of employment after agriculture in the state.

Table 10.2 shows the segregated data of the number of registered micro, small and medium enterprises in Tamil Nadu. There has been a continuous and considerable growth in all three forms of enterprises. But among them, the medium enterprises have registered a massive growth of 40 enterprises in 2007-08 to 7,177 enterprises in 2014-15 with a CAGR of 109.89 percent. During the corresponding period, the micro and small enterprises registered a CAGR of 20.51 and 49.29 percent respectively. Table 10.2 also shows the percentage of each form of enterprise to the total MSMEs in the state. Micro enterprises constitute a major share of the total MSMEs followed by small and medium enterprises. At the same time, while the percentage share of micro enterprises has been declining, the percentage share of small and medium enterprises have been increasing over the years. This reflects an increasing operational size of enterprises in the state which is beneficial in terms of more production and employment in the state. This is a good sign of the progress of MSMEs in the state of Tamil Nadu.

Table 10.2: Category-wise Number of MSMEs Registered

Year	Micro	Small	Medium	Total
2007-08	24520 (89.79)	2749 (10.07)	40 (0.15)	27309 (100)
2008-09	28232 (88.09)	3582 (11.18)	235 (0.73)	32049 (100)
2009-10	33613 (80.42)	7353 (17.59)	833 (1.99)	41799 (100)
2010-11	48730 (84.16)	8471 (14.63)	701 (1.21)	57902 (100)
2011-12	55932 (79.18)	12373 (17.52)	2334 (3.30)	70639 (100)
2012-13	55880 (61.42)	20336 (22.35)	4758 (5.23)	90974 (100)
2013-14	75660 (65.00)	34358 (29.52)	6375 (5.48)	116393 (100)
2014-15	90487 (63.23)	45440 (31.75)	7177 (5.02)	143104 (100)
CAGR	20.51	49.29	109.89	26.7

Note: Figures shown in parentheses denotes percentage to the total MSMEs.

Source: MSMED Policy Note, 2016-17, Government of Tamil Nadu.

Government Policies to Promote MSMEs in Tamil Nadu

In order to promote MSMEs in the State, the Government of Tamil Nadu provides various programmes and initiatives to encourage them to function on a sustainable basis. The Department of MSME, Government of Tamil Nadu has six major organisations under its ambit for the promotion of MSMEs in the state. They are as under:

- Commissionerate of Industries and Commerce.
- Tamil Nadu Small Industries Development Corporation Limited (TANSIDCO).
- Tamil Nadu Small Industries Corporation Limited

(TANSI).

- Entrepreneurship Development Institute (EDI).
- Tamil Nadu Small Tea Growers Industrial Cooperative Tea Factories Federation (Indcoserve).
- Salem Starch and Sago Manufacturers Service Industrial Co-operative Society Ltd. (Sagoserve).

Commissionerate of Industries and Commerce: The Commissionerate of Industries and Commerce is the State level agency that provides all escort and hand holding support to entrepreneurs through District Industries Centres (DICs). Under the control of this Commissionerate, DICs are functioning in all the 32 Districts of Tamil Nadu. DICs offices in districts give support facilities to industrial enterprises by providing a variety of services like identification of viable activities, preparation of project profiles, obtaining financial assistance from various banks/financial institutions, statutory clearances from Government departments, sanction and disbursement of eligible subsidies and obtaining payments in delayed cases.

TANSIDCO: Tamil Nadu Small Industries Development Corporation Limited (TANSIDCO) was established by the Government of Tamil Nadu in 1970 to assist and promote the interests of MSMEs in the state. It takes pro-active steps towards the development of industrial estates and associated social infrastructure, and promotion of cluster and common facility centres for MSMEs. Further, it is rendering its help in purchasing of industrial inputs and providing managerial and manufacturing practices, acquiring capital and assisting in marketing of manufactured products for MSMEs in the State. Currently, TANSIDCO is maintaining 35 industrial estates created by Government of Tamil Nadu and 59 industrial estates established on its own (Performance Budget 2016-17, MoMSMED, GoTN).

TANSI: The Tamil Nadu Small Industries Corporation Limited popularly known as TANSI, was formed in the year 1965 to take over the small-scale units under the control of the

Department of Industries and Commerce and was registered under the Companies Act, 1956. TANSI has at present 24 manufacturing units in Tamil Nadu, manufacturing different products like paints, civil interior works, baby weighing bar scales, etc. It supplies various types of classroom furniture items required by schools and colleges and line materials to Tamil Nadu Electricity Board (TNEB), spirit based products to Tamil Nadu Medical Services Corporation and hand pumps and spares required for drinking water supply etc. to panchayats and district collectorates.

EDI: The Entrepreneurship Development Institute (EDI), was constituted by the Government of Tamil Nadu as a 'not-for-profit society' in November 2001, primarily to fulfil the entrepreneurship training requirements in the State and to promote MSMEs in Tamil Nadu. Entrepreneurship development is a key aspect of employment generation and equitable economic growth. On that account, from inception until March 2016, EDI has conducted various training programmes in areas of fashion garments, food and fruit processing, web designing, hardware maintenance and networking, leather products, servicing of household electrical appliances, two wheeler repair, welding, etc. benefiting almost 1 lakh candidates which is a reasonably good achievement.

INDCOSERVE: Tamil Nadu Small Tea Growers Industrial Cooperative Tea Factories Federation called 'INDCOSERVE' was established in 1965 at Coonoor, to market the products of member tea factories to get better prices. Besides, it provides various services to the Indco Tea Factories such as warehouse facilities at Coonoor, Coimbatore and Cochin, supply of fertilizers, supply of jute bags for packing of teas, machinery spares, and other inputs to the small tea grower/members through the Indco Tea Factories. At present, 15 Industrial Cooperative Tea Factories are functioning in Nilgiris District with a membership of 24,935 and it sells Ooty Tea through public distribution system in the State (Directorate of Industries and Commerce, Government of Tamil Nadu).

SAGOSERVE: The Salem Starch and Sago Manufacturers Service Industrial Cooperative Society known as 'SAGOSERVE' was established in 1981 at Salem with the objective of helping sago and starch manufacturers of Tapioca growing districts by way of marketing their products thereby ensuring fair and remunerative prices for them. About 70,000 workers in the SSI industrial units and 5 lakh agricultural labourers engaged in planting the tapioca tubers are provided with employment through SAGOSERVE (Directorate of Industries and Commerce, Government of Tamil Nadu).

In this way, these major Government organizations of Tamil Nadu have implemented a variety of programmes related to the promotion, development and modernisation of industries, up-gradation of technology and quality control by way of providing financial assistance, technical support and guidance to the micro, small and medium enterprises. This has ensured the economic development of the state.

Special Schemes for Aspiring Entrepreneurs in the State: The Government of Tamil Nadu has implemented two schemes exclusively for the benefit of the young populace in the state. They are New Entrepreneur-cum-Enterprises Development Scheme (NEEDS) and Unemployed Youth Employment Generation Programme (UYEGP).

New Entrepreneur-cum-Enterprises Development Scheme (NEEDS): This new scheme is being implemented from 2012 onwards for assisting educated and aspiring youth in the state to become first generation entrepreneurs. The selected entrepreneurs are being assisted to prepare their business plans and help to tie up with financial institutions to set up their new business ventures.

Unemployed Youth Employment Generation Programme (UYEGP): The Government of Tamil Nadu has introduced the scheme called Unemployed Youth Employment Generation Programme (UYEGP) with an objective of mitigating the unemployment problems of socially and economically weaker sections of the society, particularly the educated unemployed youth to become self employed. Under the scheme, the youth shall set up a manufacturing or service enterprise with a project cost up to ₹ 5 lakh and ₹ 3 lakh respectively with subsidy assistance of the State Government of up to 25 percent of the project cost.

Prime Minister Employment Generation Programme (PMEGP): The Centrally sponsored Prime Minister Employment Generation Programme (PMEGP) is also being implemented in Tamil Nadu to empower the entrepreneurs for setting up of micro enterprises. The scheme provides loan assistance of ₹ 25 lakh for setting up of manufacturing enterprises and ₹ 10 lakh for setting up of service enterprises.

The number of youth, women and differently-abled that have benefited from these three schemes are given in Table 10.3.

Table 10.3: Beneficiaries from NEEDS, UYEGP and PMEGP

Year	NEEDS*		UYEGP		PMEGP	
	No. of projects	Margin money (₹ lakh)	No. of projects	Margin money (₹ lakh)	No. of projects	Margin money (₹ lakh)
Youth						
2011-12	-	-	4750	1314.17	1560	2909.03
2012-13	218	2385.76	4804	1466.31	1316	2258.4
2013-14	456	4334.82	4657	1499.53	1036	2366.9
2014-15	172	995.42	3465	1817.7	1256	2827.68
Women						
2011-12	-	-	1187	367.96	548	1010.42
2012-13	91	891.8	1441	439.89	484	803.99
2013-14	146	1197.2	1536	494.84	352	751.79
2014-15	60	334.64	848	441.12	457	974.79
Differently-abled						
2011-12	-	-	95	26.28	29	17.26
2012-13	-	-	96	29.33	21	16.82
2013-14	-	-	93	29.99	14	23.18
2014-15	-	-	69	36.35	13	14.62

*NEEDS Scheme introduced from 2012-13.
Source: State Industrial Profile, 2014-15, Tamil Nadu, MoMSMEs.

From Table 10.3, it can be clearly seen that among these three schemes, UYEGP has sanctioned more number of projects than NEEDS and PMEGP in all the years. But when it comes to disbursement of margin money, the other two schemes outperform UYEGP. For women beneficiaries, the NEEDS has sanctioned more money than PMEGP during the first two years of its formation but then in 2014-15, it fell drastically from ₹ 1,197.2 lakh in 2013-14 to ₹ 334.64 in 2014-15. Further, the PMEGP shows a declining trend in money sanctioned to the women beneficiaries during the period 2011-12 to 2013-14, but it improved in 2014-15. A very important concern exposed from the Table is the level of benefits acquired by the differently-abled beneficiaries in terms of both number of projects and the money sanctioned.

During these years, the UYEGP has sanctioned 95 (2011-12), 96 (2012-13), 93 (2013-14) and 69 (2014-15) projects and number of beneficiaries from PMEGP are only 29, 21, 14 and 13 in respective years. During these years, the money sanctioned by UYEGP for differently-abled ranges between 26 and 36 lakh and it ranges between 14 and 23 lakh in PMEGP. Moreover, in all these years, there was no beneficiary at all from NEEDS scheme, which calls for immediate attention from the policymakers and concerned authorities.

Problems Faced by MSMEs

Despite the commendable growth of MSMEs in the state, the sector faces a number of problems and constraints in their path of progress. A report of Reserve Bank of India, titled, ‘Working Group on Rehabilitation of MSMEs’ has identified the following as the top five constraints of MSMEs in India which is applicable to Tamil Nadu as well. They are the following:

Inadequate Market Linkage: MSMEs tend to have poor market access. These units often do not possess any marketing organization and therefore they suffer from a competitive disadvantage with large-scale units.

Lack of Infrastructure: Limited access to infrastructure such as power, water and roads increases operational costs for

MSMEs and makes their businesses uncompetitive.

Inadequate Finance: Of the many challenges impeding the growth and development of MSMEs, inadequate and timely unavailability of financial resources is the key bottleneck that makes these enterprises vulnerable.

Lack of Managerial Competence: MSMEs largely comprise of first-generation entrepreneurs, who have limited training on resource planning, capital management and labour management, which inhibits the growth of these enterprises.

Obsolete technology: These enterprises have limited awareness about new technologies, or the technology financing schemes. A low technology base results in low productivity, which makes these enterprises incompetent.

Apart from these, the sector also faces the following problems:

- High cost of credit.
- Non-availability of labour with required skills at affordable cost.
- Collateral requirements.
- Procurement of raw materials at competitive cost.
- Problems of storage, designing, packaging and product display.
- Lack of access to global markets.
- Multiplicity of labour laws and complicated procedures associated with compliance of such laws.
- Absence of a suitable mechanism which enables the quick revival of viable sick enterprises and allows unviable entities to close down speedily.

Suggestions

- Success of an enterprise irrespective of the scale of operation depends mainly upon the competitive nature of its products, managerial efficiency and process technology. Therefore, the government and financial institutions need to play a dynamic role by providing technical guidance and timely credit to MSMEs considering the limited resources of small entrepreneurs.

- Effective steps should be taken by the government to develop entrepreneurial knowledge and skill to raise level of motivation particularly to women to start and run an enterprise.
- Free training facilities and proper technical education should be provided in all fields of enterprises especially to women and differently-abled.
- Government should encourage modernisation and up-gradation of technology in MSMEs for having competitive edge in the wake of changing economic environment.
- MSMEs should be made aware of various credit facilities, financial incentives and subsidies. Steps must be taken to ensure access to information for availing benefit of various promotional Government schemes.
- During times of natural disasters like floods, the MSMEs get badly affected since they do not get relief funds. This is due to a technicality in the provisions of the National Disaster Relief Fund (NDRF) which does not include MSMEs. A provision needs to be added for distribution of relief to MSMEs as well by the Centre, so that the state can then utilise these funds for immediate disbursal of relief and help our small entrepreneurs get back to their feet faster.
- Government should take steps to develop markets in rural and semi-urban areas so that these MSMEs can sell their products easily in the nearest markets. Also, more fairs and exhibitions should be arranged for MSME products.
- Government should conduct evaluation of the working of the various schemes and also continuously review the procedures to ensure simplification to start and run the enterprises. For instance, the different application and guidelines forms should be made available in regional languages. This will enable people at all levels to easily understand the Government policies for their enterprises.
- Steps can be taken to provide incentives for adoption of

low cost environment-friendly technologies.

Conclusion

On the whole, in spite of the various problems that come in the way of progress, the MSME sector has performed exceptionally well and has made significant contributions to employment generation and economic development of Tamil Nadu and also for India. In this setting, given the size and scope of the sector, it is imperative for the Governments at Central and State level to create effective strategies to address the mentioned issues through a combination of strong policy measures, skill development and infrastructure facilities. Further, well-rounded fiscal support by the government and financial institutions will help the MSME sector to grow at a steady pace and contribute to economic development considerably higher than it is doing currently.

References

Chandraiah, M. and R. Vani (2014), "The Prospects and Problems of MSMEs Sector in India: An Analytical Study", *International Journal of Business and Management Invention,* 3(8), 27-40.

Das, S.K. (2014), "Growth and Prospects of MSMEs in Odisha: An Analytical Approach", *Odisha Review,* 102-111, available at: http://odisha.gov.in/e-magazine/Orissareview/2014/Feb-March/engpdf/102-111.pdf.

International Finance Corporation (2012), "Micro, Small and Medium Enterprise Finance in India", International Finance Corporation (IFC), World Bank Group.

Katyal, Ashu and Betsy Xaviour (2015), "A Study on MSMEs' Role in Propelling Economic Development of India and a Discussion on Current HR Issues in MSMEs in India", *International Journal of Scientific and Research Publications,* 5(2).

Micro, Small and Medium Enterprises Department (2016), "Annual Report, 2015-16", Ministry of Micro, Small and Medium Enterprises, Government of India.

Micro, Small and Medium Enterprises Department (2016), "Policy Note, 2016-17", Ministry of Micro, Small and Medium Enterprises, Government of Tamil Nadu.

MSME Development Institute (2015), "State Industrial Profile, 2014-15, Tamil Nadu", Ministry of Micro, Small and Medium Enterprises, Government of India.

Reserve Bank of India (2008), "Report of the Working Group on Rehabilitation of MSMEs", Reserve Bank of India, available at: https://www.rbi.org.in/scripts/BS_PressReleaseDisplay.aspx?prid=18216.

11

Women Entrepreneurs in Micro, Small and Medium Enterprises in Odisha

Ashutosh Dash

Rationale

Women in India are in no way inferior to men in all walks of life. They can prove to be good entrepreneurs as men are in the country. Since they represent 50 percent of the country's population, it is essential to tap their potential by encouraging their participation in MSMEs. Women's participation in entrepreneurship is poor, mainly because of the problems associated with their gender roles. There is a need to emphasize the problems faced by women and to plan support systems that will enhance entrepreneurship of women in India. Women entrepreneurs have been making a significant impact in all segments of the economy in Canada, Great Britain, Germany, Australia, US, and so in India.

The Government of India has defined women entrepreneurs, based on women participation in equity and employment of a business enterprise. It is a group of women or single women running an enterprise or company in order to earn profit. Informal sector plays a vital role in terms of providing employment opportunity to a large segment of the working force in the country, especially women. Although this sector offers low remuneration, women are compelled to join this sector due to poverty and lack of opportunities in the formal sector due to their illiteracy and skills. In the era of liberalization, privatization, and globalization, today's world is changing at an unprecedented pace. Economic transformations appear to be taking place everywhere as countries convert from command to demand economies and dictatorships move towards democratic systems. These changes have created economic opportunities for women who want to start and run enterprises on their own.

"Phula Badi" (Flower shaped handmade black gram dumpling) produced in Keonjhar is famous for its subtle crisp texture and delectable taste. In some parts of Keonjhar, women are involved in the production of badi (handmade black gram dumpling) for earning additional livelihood. More than 200 SHGs of Keonjhar are involved in this activity. Due to its limited shelf life, SHGs were unable to produce in larger quantities and hold these for business for a longer period. In order to provide more income to these producers, a pilot project was undertaken by ORMAS in the year 2008-09 to mechanize the production system.

Under this initiative, infrastructural supports like production unit, manual dryer, packaging machine etc. were provided at Dimbo village of Sadar block in Keonjhar district. To manage the unit professionally, 144 women members of 12 SHGs were imparted with basic orientation as well as skill training. A dedicated federation was formed under Maa Mission Shakti program and is now in operation. When it comes to empowering women, the district of Keonjhar has come up as the hub of providing a steady income to hundreds of women through the manufacturing of phula badi.

There are a number of SHGs operating in Badi-making business at Keonjhar district namely, Sri Maa Mission Shakti at Dimbo village, Sri Chandi SHG at Atopur, Maa Gouri SHG at Bistapal village, Maa Tarini SHG at Kamaragada, Maa Durga SHG at Khuntapada, Dibya Shakti SHG at Khuntapada, Maa Santoshi SHG at Bistapal village, Maa Sidha Kali SHG at Old town, Bamana Raja SHG at Atopur, Karma Thakurani SHG at Atopur, Maa Laxmi SHG at Kashipur and many more. It is a black gram preparation usually fried or roasted and consumed as a side-dish. It is prepared from a wide range of ingredients; the most relished being 'phula badi' made from black gram.

The 'phula badi' prepared here is extremely famous all over the state and is recently gaining popularity beyond the border as well. It is widely believed that the crispy, crunchy dumpling marked its beginning in the districts of the Keonjhar among the tribal populace. Even today, it is offered as *prasad* to the deities in many temples in Keonjhar. Ten varieties of the badis, for example, are offered to the deity in the Baldev Jew temple in Keonjhar district on the occasion of *makar sankranti*. Apart from this, it also makes it way out of traditional Odia homes to be sold in shops and outlets. Badi has become a source of income for many families. It is estimated that today, around 850 families in Keonjhar district alone earn their livelihood from badi-making.

The entire process has taken commercial proportion and bigger players in the market are turning on to mechanized production of badi to meet the growing demands. What is heartening is the fact that now badis are in demand not only in other states but also in countries like US and China. The demand for Keonjhar phula badi is all over India. Apart from other industries, the phula badi business has gained the status of small-scale and cottage industries in the district. The local people of Keonjhar district give a packet of badis as a token to whoever visits the area.

Review of Literature

The Japanese delegation, which visited India (1961), [1] found that most of the facilities and concessions provided were in excess of their requirements and warned that it would lead to continuous dependence of these units on the government.

Prasad (1974) [2] in his study highlighted that small-scale industrial sector in India is small only in size but big in achievements.

A study conducted by Bhati (1976) [3] states that in the majority of cases, units outside the industrial estates, showed higher rates of surplus.

Graham Bannock [1981] [4] presents a vivid picture of the

practical problems of individual small businesses, showing how they relate to the wider issues of economic policy. He believes the release of the economic dynamisms inherent in the small business sector could help to generate social and economic change needed for the resumption of inflation-free growth.

Roy Roth Well and Water Zegveld (1982) [5] reveal that SMEs have been and in general, continue to be, technologically innovative. Technology-based new SMEs play an important part in the emergence of new technology and in economic growth of SME, particularly, young technology-based SMEs also make an exceptional contribution to employment creation. Independent SMEs, and their larger counterparts, does represent an important vehicle for regional regeneration.

Narayana Reddy (1983) [6] in his doctoral thesis reports that SSI units are to equip themselves with better and improved methods of marketing, disseminated through proper training programmes conducted by the Institute of Marketing, which may be started exclusively. Hence, there is a need for creating the Institute of Marketing for small industry at national level.

Ram Vepa (1983) [7] in his study reports that over the last 25 years a network of institutions and policies has been developed in the country but not all of them have been successful. But taken in totality, they have provided a well-organized framework in which small and cottage industries have been allowed to grow.

Vinayak Shankarrao Bhoyar (1984) [8] states that programme of co-operative industrial estates coupled with co-operatives in other related fields is a powerful instrument, which possesses the capacity to transform the backward areas into advanced ones.

The Task Force on Small-Scale Industries (1984) [9] found that available subsidies and concessions are not distributed to eligible units at the right time. Such assistance announced by the government is delayed for several reasons such as delay in issuing detailed orders, inadequacy of budget provisions etc.

Envying Chita and Carl Lied Holm [1985] [10] in a comprehensive study of SSI in Sierra Leone provide a new insight into the role of SSIs in providing production, employment and earning opportunities. Besides giving an overview of the role of the rural and urban Industry in Siena Leone, the determinants of the demand for and supply of SSI products are examined.

The Report of the Sub-Group on Small-Scale Industries for the Seventh Plan (1985) [11] had found that the efforts of the government have not met with the same degree of success in different parts of the country nor have they removed the basic weaknesses of the small-scale sector.

Ashok Kumar Singh [1985] [12] in his thesis made an effort to study the incentives and assistance provided by the government and the infrastructure facilities available in Bihar. A brief account of the potentialities and prospects of SSIs in Bihar is also given.

Tara Nand Singh and Devandra Thakar (1986) [13] reveal that the fundamental problem of industrial development in India is the problem of transplanting and acclimatizing the fruits of technology so as to raise the whole level of productivity.

Nisar Ahmad [1937] [14] has made an effort to critically examine, both at micro and macro levels, the operational and other problems of the small-scale and cottage industries in India with special reference to the state of Jammu and Kashmir.

Sandesara (1988) [15] made a study of assistance programmes for small-scale industries. The study revealed that units producing items in the reserved list did not show superior performance over other units, mainly because the easy entry for new small-scale units had intensified the competition among the small units.

Ram Vepa (1988) [16] in his study discusses the growth of small-scale industry, organizational structure, some key issues, and field planning for small-scale industry and its prospects for 1990s.

Nasir Tyabji (1989) [17] analyses the structure of small-scale Industries and role of small industry policy as a component of the Indian development process and changes in the structure of industry and nature of small enterprise development.

Dash and others [1990] [18] in their study undertaken in Balasore district in Orissa attempted to analyze the operational problems in launching SSI units. They conclude that although policies are good, often delay in implementation and faulty implementation upsets an entrepreneur's plan and in many cases leads to a standstill production.

Theophilus (1990) [19] observed that the operation of SSIs in India and Nigeria encounter similar incidences and show the same environmental characteristics for their progress. He suggests that there should be a separate ministry exclusively for SSIs at the central level headed by a central minister in both countries.

Sharma (1990) [20] in his study made an effort to make an overview of sports goods industry, micro industry of selected centres, problems at different levels, role of institutions and future perspectives.

In a study conducted by Berry, Albert and Mazumdar (1991) [21], they found that small-scale industry has been instrumental in the successful development of MSME.

Objectives, Data and Research Methodology

1. To analyse the economic and social gains derived by both SHGs and non-SHG women "badi" workers.
2. To examine the socio-economic profile of women badi workers in the study area.
3. To investigate the promotional role and various activities of women self-help groups.

The present paper is based on primary and secondary data. Secondary data is collected from Mission Shakti for the time period 2005-2015, Economic Survey of Odisha and other publications. The primary data is collected through choice based questionnaire method and the study was conducted in Dhenkapur, Atopur, Old Town, Kashipur, Dimbo Village, Banspal, Harichandanpur, Jhumpura areas of Keonjhar district. The data is collected from 100 women badi workers of Keonjhar. Simple random sampling was used for selecting areas and households. The is analyzed by using different statistical tools like classification, tabulation, percentage, arithmetic mean, regression, bar charts with MS Excel and SPSS software.

Findings of the Study

1. The present study illustrates that 94.67 percent of women 'badi' workers belonging to SHGs were married and 100 percent in case of non-SHGs.
2. It was found that all the women 'badi' workers of SHGs and non-SHGs belonged to the Hindu religion and it was also found that 89.33 percent of general caste members belonged to SHGs and 68 percent in case of non-SHGs.
3. It was found that 71.33 percent of SHG 'badi' workers were illiterate—under primary and primary— and that 48 percent in the case of non-SHGs were illiterate.
4. It was found that 69.33 percent of SHG badi workers lived in nuclear families and 60 percent of non-SHG badi workers lived in nuclear families.
5. It was found that 93.33 percent of SHG badi workers had an annual income between ₹ 30,000-₹ 50,000.

Suggestions

1. The Government should come forward to provide minimum entrepreneurship program through District Industries Centre. This may pave the way for practical and technical training for the 'badi' workers in Keonjhar. It will develop self-confidence, self-esteem, courage and risk

factor among them.

2. Training programmes should be designed in such manners that 'badi' workers can benefit out of their strengths and overcome their weaknesses and should provide special assistance for selection of service so that 'badi' workers can be in a position to perceive and respond to various profitable opportunities.
3. Government should organise micro credit camps and credit-cum-recovery camps to facilitate early completion of the formalities required for sanction of loans to avoid hardships to the 'badi' workers.
4. Training in book-keeping, accounts, fund management and other financial matters related to the SHGs are essential to make the members competent enough to deal with the increasing volume of transactions.
5. Proper marketing facilities and sales exhibition should be provided by the Government to the 'badi' workers.

Conclusions

Women's empowerment is a continuous process. The development of 'badi' in Keonjhar should be taken in the broader framework of women empowerment. The small-scale and cottage industry in Keonjhar puts efforts towards the all-round development of each and every section of women involved in badi-making activity in Keonjhar. Badi-making industry in Keonjhar is responsible for empowering women by way of promoting self-reliance, self-confidence, self-independence and by providing educational training and skill-based programmes conducted from time-to-time by government and NGOs to realize their fundamental rights. Badi-making industry in Keonjhar has made women financially stable to such an extent that after taking their rightful share of their livelihood, they are contributing to the societal cause also. Hence, women empowerment is the need of the hour in Badi-making industry.

Endnotes

1. Ministry of Commerce and Industry, Report of the Japanese Delegation, Government of India, New Delhi, 1961.
2. C.S. Prasad, "Small Sectors: Big Achievements", *Yojana*, March 15, 1974, p. 8.
3. G.S. Bhati, "Industrial Estates: An Evaluation", University of Bombay, 1976.
4. Graham Bannock, "The Economics of Small Firms: Return from the Wilderness", Oxford: Basil Blackwell, 1981.
5. Roy Roth Well and Walter Zegveld, "Innovation and Small and Medium Sized Firm: Their Role in Employment and in Economic Change", Frances Printer, London, 1982.
6. P. Narayana Reddy, "Marketing Problems in Small-scale Industries", Ph.D. thesis, Sri Krishnadevaraya University Anantapur, 1983.
7. Ram K. Vepa, "Small Industry Development Programme", Indian Institute of Public Administration, New Delhi, 1983.
8. Vinayak Shankarrao Bhoyar, "The Role of Co-operative Industrial Estates in the Development of Small-scale Industries in Maharashtra State", Ph.D. thesis, Nagpur University, 1984.
9. State Planning Board, "Report of High-Level Committee on Industry Trade and Power", Vol. II, Government of Kerala, Trivandrum, 1984.
10. Envy Vinna Chuta and C. Liedholun, "Employment Growth in SSI Industry: Empirical Evidence and Assessment from Sierra Leone", The Macmillan Press Ltd., 1985.
11. Sub-group on Small-Scale Industries, "Report of the Working Group on Small-Scale Industries for the Seventh Plan", Government of India, New Delhi, 1985, p.10.
12. Ashok Kumar *Singh* "Problems and Prospects of Small-scale Industries in Bihar: A Critical Study", Ph.D. thesis, Bihar University, 1985.
13. Tara Nand Singh Tarun and Devandra Thakur, "Small-scale Industries and Indian Economic Development", Deep and Deep Publications, New Delhi, 1986.
14. Nisar Ahmad, "Problems and Management of Small-scale and Cottage Industries", Deep and Deep Publications, New Delhi, 1987.
15. J.C. Sandesara, "Small Industry Development Programme in India-Efficiency Explanation and Lessons: Some Field Study", in K.B. Suri (ed.), op. cit., pp. 227-298; see also, J.C. Sandesara (1988: b)

"Industrial Framework for Promoting Small-Scale Industries in India", *Asian Development Review*, Vol. VI, No. 2, 1988, pp. 10-40.
16. Ram K. Vepa, "Modem Small Industry in India: Problems and Prospects", Sage Publications, New Delhi, 1958.
17. Nasir Tyabji, "The Small Industry Policy in India", Oxford University Press, Oxford, 1989.
18. Sidhartha Shankar, Jyotinnayee Kar, and Arabinda Sarangi, "Operational and Government Support in Promoting SSI in Balasore District of Orissa", SEDEME 17 No. 3, 1990, pp. 31-37.
19. Theophilus-o-Uche, "A Study of Impact of the Government's Promotional and Protective Measures on Small-scale Industries Development: A Comparative Analysis of India and Nigeria", Ph.D. thesis, Nagpur University, 1990.
20. J.P Sharma, "Small-scale Industry: Problems and Prospects", Anmol Publications, New Delhi, 1990.
21. Berry Albert, Mazumdar Dipak, "Small-scale Industry in the Asian Specific Region", *Asia Pacific Economic Literature*, 5(2) September 1991, pp. 35-67.

References

Anselm, M. (1992), "Women Entrepreneurs: Agents of Social Change", *Entrepreneurship Innovation and Change,* Vol. 2, No. 1.

Berger, Guillamon M. (2006), "Women's Ventures: Assistance to the Informal Sector in Latin America", Kumarian Press Inc.

Bhatia, B.S. (2004), "New Industrial Entrepreneurs: Their Origins and Problems", *Journal of General Management,* 2(10).

Bhattacharjee, S.K. and M.M.P. Akhowri (1975), "Profile of Small Industry Entrepreneurs", SEDME, Vol. 1, No. 2.

Birley, S. (2009), "Female Entrepreneurs: Are They Really Any Sifferent", *Journal of Small Business Management*, Vol. 27, No. 1.

Chandra, V.A.S. and D. Kajipet (1988), "Women Entrepreneurship in India: A Retrospect and Prospect", in C.S. Lakshmi (ed.), 'Development of Women Entrepreneurship in India', Discovery Publishing House, New Delhi.

Chowdhury, H. Md. (2000), "Performance of Small Entrepreneurs: The Case of Dholai-Khal", SEDME, 27(2), June.

Das, M. (1999), "Women Entrepreneurs from Southern India: An Exploratory Study", *The Journal of Entrepreneurship*, Vol. 8, No. 2 Sage Publications, New Delhi.

Donkels and Dupton (2009), "Gender and Growth of Micro Enterprise",

Small Enterprise Development, 2(1).

Gopakumar, K. (2008), "The Entrepreneur in Economic Thought: A Thematic Overview", *The Journal of Entrepreneurship*, 4(1).

Rao, C.H. (1995), "DWCRA: A Means of Women's Empowerment-Case Study of a DWCRA Group", SEDME, Vol. CCII, No. 4, December.

Schwartz, E.B. (2008), "Entrepreneurship: A New Female Frontier", *Journal of Contemporary Business*, 28-29.

Venkatapathy, R. (2006), "Getting Women into Business", *Manushi*, No. 95, July-August, 27-28.

12

Rural Handicraft Artisans

Keya (Das) Ghosh

Introduction

Micro entrepreneurs, apart from being low in technical and marketing knowledge, are also unfamiliar with contemporary marketing issues like quality, delivery schedule, packaging and labelling, pricing, market research, promotion and advertising and after sales service, etc. [1] Consequently, they have failed to sustain in the market, featured with stiff competition and the advent of large scale retailers and MNCs. The failure of the rural producers not only condescend the growth in the agriculture and allied sector in India, which registered a growth of around 3 percent in the last four decades, but also whoop coughing governments' policies of poverty eradication and inclusive growth.

Rationale of the Study and Research Objectives

The present research is confined to rural micro entrepreneurs and small business communities of West Bengal who deal with handicrafts and handlooms. Rural producers, suppliers and artisans, along with the age old traditional knowledge and skill are not only cherished in this land of Nobel laureate Rabindranath Tagore, but is also rich in natural resources and cultural diversity. The rich and diverse cultural heritage, traditional crafts and customs of the state bears signs of neglect, though a massive market potentiality is present for these traditional artifacts, rural products and services. Among others, the ethnic origin, indigenous design and folkloric appearance are the major attributes for which these artifacts and products, including handicrafts, toys, apparels and food products, home furnishing etc., have attracted a premium in the present day aesthetic market.

The research is cantered on the conceptions promulgated by late Professor C.K. Prahalad in his book "The Fortune at the Bottom of the Pyramid". He opined, "The poor must be active, informed, and involved producers to result in co-creating a market around the needs of the population, for the reduction of poverty". [2]

Despite all odds, the Indian rural market has revealed some remarkable trends and developments. Four consecutive years of positive growth in rural GDP has not just boosted sentiments but also the ability to purchase. The power play of MGNREGS, farm loan waiver, more than 40 percent hike in support prices of crops over the last two years, higher percentage of disposable income in rural vis-à-vis urban areas due to negligible expenses on house rent and taxes, corporate engagement etc. have begun to have a small but definitive impact on rural incomes (Kahn, 1962). [3] Big corporates are considering rural markets as the next big opportunity. But on the flip side, the rural producers/artisans have not been furthered which could quicken the progress of rural marketing. Inclusive growth cannot be accomplished unless welfare touches the last person of the country. [4]

The contemporary economic development approach revolves around the concept of entrepreneurship for the betterment of rural livelihood and long-run sustenance (Drabensott et al., 2003; [5] Merrett and Gruidl, 2000). [6] The sustainability and viability of local economic systems, directly knotted with the uses of indigenous entrepreneurial skills and knowledge through collective efforts of associates of the rural communities, can be instrumental to a sustainable livelihood for them to realize the inclusive rural growth (Flora et al., 1992; [7] Kinsley, 1997; [8] Miller and Besser, 2000). [9]

The entrepreneurship in rural India has been dampened by impediments like rigid caste system, absence of education and awareness, poor infrastructure facilities etc. In the last few years, rural entrepreneurial growth has been limited by a number of factors, including limited local demand, and poor access to extra-regional markets, low density of floating population, deficiency in opportunities for networking, inadequate access to and unfamiliarity with ICT, and restricted accessibility to capital (Nerys, F. et al., 2006). [10]

The achievement of success by the rural enterprises depends on two key functions i.e. effective marketing, and internal resource generation including judicious use of finance. Too much production orientation is a common fallacy or fiascos of some rural entrepreneurial efforts. Marketing function involves the whole lot which could be imperative to remain and lead in the market. It involves constant interface and cooperation with all stakeholders (Reardon et al., 1998). [11]

The promotion of rural non-farm enterprises is the tool with the potentiality to absorb surplus and additional farm labour, to provide a sustained employment, regulate capital formation and uses, impassion rural development and reduce rural poverty (Christensen and Lacroix, 1997). [12]

The present study is confined to non-farm sector and focuses more on problems of rural producers such as artisans and handicraftsmen. These producers have not been able to improve their economic conditions because of slow adaptability, lack of education, raw material unavailability, poor quality and productivity, and lack of market intelligence, poor managerial skills and many more to add (Taori and Singh, 1995). [13] They also lack understanding of the local demand pattern of the area, market dynamics, market channel, price fluctuations, and value addition possibilities, which can help them develop a comprehensive intervention plan based on market realities. This is due to the present market efficacies and complicacies (Kashyap, P. and Raut, S., 2006) [14]

Against this backdrop, the present study makes an attempt to understand and analyse the problems and issues of rural micro entrepreneurs and producers from various parts of the

Indian subcontinent in general and West Bengal in particular.

Research Design and Methodology

The study was restricted to rural sectors of West Bengal. Bankura and Bishnupur were selected for the purpose of study. These areas are economically backward regions. The indigenous rural artisans in these two districts are involved in terracotta and handloom activities, which earn a spot in the cultural map of India for its conspicuous designs and artistic handiworks.

The exploratory research design was preferred for the present study as the main purpose of the study was to explore current status of marketing and the related problems of the rural producers, suppliers and artisans of the state of West Bengal. Data sources are both from primary and secondary sources. A total of 75 pilot-tested schedules were administrated on rural micro producers of two districts undertaken for the study, out of which researchers could collect 50 useful filled schedules, which were furthered for the analysis.

The non-disguised structured questionnaire administered for the study has two parts. First part contains questions related to demographic personal information about the respondents. The latter part which addresses the main objectives contains 27 statements related to different problems faced by the responding entrepreneurs. The degree of each statement was determined using a four-point rating scale viz., frequently (3), sometimes (2), rarely (1) and never (0). The 27 statements were grouped under four critical factors' categories viz., product related problems, price related problems, distribution related problems, and promotion related problems. Cronbach's Alpha Test was conducted over the multi-item scale presented through the schedules for its reliability. The calculated value of alpha was 0.795 for this instrument, which indicated the instrument as reliable.

Empirical Analysis

Demographic Analysis: It was witnessed from the field

study that 82 percent were males (41) and 18 percent were females (09). A majority of them were in the age group of 25-40 years (45, 90 percent) and only rest 5 (10 percent) were above the age of 40 years. The higher middle age group among the respondents indicates that they have opposite business experience and also possess future potentiality. With respect to the educational qualifications, nearly one-fourth of sample micro entrepreneurs (12, 24 percent) were intermediate pass and 30 (60 percent) of them were primary educated. 16 percent of the respondents (8) were either illiterate or without any formal education. 52 percent of the sampled artisans (26) had more than 5-10 years', 40 percent (20) in between 0 to 5 years' and the rest (4, 8 percent) with more than 10 years' of experience in their respective fields of business.

Marketing Problems Faced by the Sampled Micro Entrepreneurs: Through the schedule and primary data collected, the four critical factors of marketing mix viz., product, price, promotion and place of these rural micro entrepreneurs under study were identified for understanding their marketing related practices and problems (José de la Paz, Hernández Girón et al., 2007). The schedule with twenty seven statements related to various aspects of marketing related problems, were administered to 50 respondents and each response was enumerated on a four-point scale (0-3) viz., frequently (3), sometimes (2), rarely (1) and never (0). The highest possible score for each of the statement of the critical factor (CF) was three. It is very well understood from Table 12.1 that there is a huge variation among different problems within the same element of marketing problems, as the mean is varied from element to element. The major individual problem areas in each four critical factor areas are:

1. Packaging and labelling of the products.
2. Product pricing methodology.
3. Selling product to middlemen.
4. Promotion and advertising issues.

The degree of problems among different critical marketing factors (CF) were also analysed and are described in Table 12.1. It is evident from the Table that product related problems with a mean score of 19.459 was the most critical factor followed by pricing related issues with a mean score of 12.558. Distribution related (mean score: 10.760) and promotion related issues (5.150) were apparently termed as less problematic factors. The apparent causes of it may be due to their selling of the produce to the middlemen rather than to the end-customers.

Apart from the primary data collected from the areas of study, there were several interviews and discussions with these rural craftsmen, artisans and producers. During different meetings with them, researchers found the following major issues and problems, which are really burgeoning with time and changing market place. Following are the major problems earmarked on the basis of the above analysis:

1. Unlike the big sales houses and production houses, the small scale micro rural producers have absolutely no budgets for customer need assessment and identification, market research and forecasting, product innovation, product standardisation, quality control, and above all, promotion and advertising. Product quality is inconsistent and non-standardised.
2. Limited access to easy availability of raw material and other factors of production are some major issues for small rural producers.
3. One of the major product related issues is the copyright and intellectual property rights of the product design and manufacturing process etc.
4. Unaware about potential new markets and limited access to these markets leads to limited capacity of the rural entrepreneurs as regards scientific pricing strategies, balance price and quality.
5. High dependency on the middlemen is a way to exploitation.

Table 12.1: Mean Score of Responses of Micro Entrepreneurs on Various Element of Marketing Problems

Critical Factors (CF)	Problem Statements of various Critical Factors	Mean	SD	Mean of CF
Product related Problems	Packaging and Labelling	2.876	0.318	**19.459**
	Protection of product from competition	2.039	0.420	
	Product handling	1.926	0.654	
	Defective products	1.287	0.878	
	Easy in availability of Raw material etc.	2.213	0.576	
	Product Quality	1.602	1.299	
	Product Design	1.685	0.467	
	Product Innovation	1.846	0.621	
	Substituted / Copycat product	2.217	0.578	
	Product Awareness	1.768	0.661	
Price related Problems	Product Pricing methodology	2.212	0.601	**12.558**
	Quality and price imbalance	1.723	0.601	
	Inability to recover the cost	1.756	0.812	
	Demand in market for the artefacts	1.961	0.202	
	Price elasticity	1.786	0.700	
	Making adequate profit	1.552	0.901	
	Customers' grumble about price	1.568	0.549	
Distribution related Problems	Selling product to middleman	2.632	0.798	**10.760**
	Selling product direct to customer	2.253	0.958	
	Financial help from middleman	1.232	0.862	
	New business provided by middleman	0.974	0.701	
	Middleman's idea for business development	0.898	0.603	
	Middleman's help for raw material sources	1.373	1.168	
	Middleman' effort to promote product	1.398	0.798	
Promotion related Problems	Promotion and advertisement issues	2.472	0.845	**5.150**
	Participation in Haat, Mela, exhibition	1.264	0.901	
	Gifting and sampling of product	1.432	0.702	
Aggregate Score				**47.927**

Source: Primary data collected from the survey in 2016 and analyzed.

Cross Relationship between the Demographic Variables and the Critical Factors of Problems Faced by the Micro Entrepreneurs

The problem related to marketing of the rural produce faced by the responding entrepreneurs from Bishnupur and Bankura districts of West Bengal have a different facet and individualistic character. The problems may vary with demographic variables like sex, educational qualifications and years of experience in the business.

While calculating the T-values against the responses for various CFs (4Ps) by the male and female respondents, it was found that both types of rural micro entrepreneurs (males and females) perceived the marketing related problems with same intensity. No significant statistical difference was recorded from the primary data, as presented in Table 12.2.

Table 12.2: T-test Scores on the Effect of Gender on Perceptions about Marketing Problems

Impacting Factors	Variables (CFs)	T-test Score	df	Significance
Gender (Male Vs. Female)	Product	1.7276	48	NS
	Price	-1.621	48	NS
	Place	- 1.413	48	NS
	Promotion	1.187	48	NS
	Aggregate	0.712	48	NS

(**SIG = significant at 1 percent, *SIG = significant at 5 percent, NS = non-significant)

Source: Primary data collected from the survey in 2016 and analysis thereafter.

Unlikely to the above inference, the relationship between the effect of educational level of the micro entrepreneurs under study has showed some significant differences i.e., with respect to the price and place critical factors, when the data collected were put to the test of ANOVA. Both the CFs showed a difference of perception about problems along the educational level. Since pricing practices are very technical in nature, the difference in educational level made some perceptional dissimilarities. The choice of marketing channel and middlemen, communication and bargaining capability, etc. were highly affected by the levels of educational, which was clearly evidenced by the test of ANOVA, as presented in Table 12.3.

Table 12.3: ANOVA Scores on the Effect of Difference of Educational Level on Perceptions about Marketing Problems

Impacting Factors	Variables (CFs)	F	df	Significance
Education Level (Illiterate Vs. Primary Vs. Intermediate)	Product	3.182	2, 47	NS
	Price	4.823	2, 47	*SIG
	Place	4.998	2, 47	*SIG
	Promotion	0.398	2, 47	NS
	Aggregate	1.341	2, 47	NS

(**SIG = significant at 1 percent, *SIG = significant at 5 percent, NS = non-significant)

Source: Primary data collected from the survey in 2016 and analysis thereafter.

Putting the collected responses of the micro entrepreneurs under study with respect to the perceived marketing problems against the variable years of experience in the business through ANOVA, the following inferences were drawn. A statistical significant difference at 1 percent significance level was found across the years of experience when the aggregate responses about the marketing problem were taken into consideration. The association in the business activities for a higher period led to mastering the finer ideas in marketing activities. With respect to the individual critical factors, the statistical significant differences were found with price and place, at 1 percent significance level (Table 12.4).

Findings of the Study

The present study was undertaken with the aim to study different problems faced by the micro rural entrepreneurs of West Bengal and to analyse the impact of the demographic variables like sex, educational attainment and the years of experience on various marketing related problems grouped under four critical factors viz., product, price, place and promotion (4Ps). The following inference was drawn from the above analysis.

Table 12.4: ANOVA Scores on the Effect of Years of Experience on Perceptions about Marketing Problems

Impacting factors	Variables (CFs)	F	df	Significance
Years of Experience (0-5 yrs Vs. 5-10 years Vs. Above10 years)	Product	3.182	2, 47	NS
	Price	4.823	2, 47	**SIG
	Place	4.998	2, 47	**SIG
	Promotion	0.398	2, 47	NS
	Aggregate	1.341	2, 47	**SIG

(**SIG = significant at 1 percent, *SIG = significant at 5 percent, NS = non-significant)

Source: Primary data collected from the survey in 2016 and analysis thereafter.

1. The worst problems faced by the micro entrepreneurs were with respect to packaging and labelling of the products, product pricing methodology, selling product to the middlemen and promotion and advertisement issues.
2. The next level of problems were with respect to availability and accessibility of factors of production, lack of awareness about intellectual property rights, selling product to the ultimate customers while defying the stiff competition, and making sample products.
3. All micro rural entrepreneurs faced similar types of problems irrespective of the gender.
4. The education level and the years of experience played a vital role with respect to the intensity of the problems.

Suggestive Measures

Rural micro entrepreneurship supported by a strong marketing infrastructure is a critical constituent for inclusive rural growth. Basing on the observations, interviews with the stakeholders like association members of the entrepreneurs, DIC officials, and staff members of facilitating agencies (banks and NGOs), the middlemen, and marketers etc., the following strategic measures are proposed to rejuvenate the eminence of these rural producers and increase their prospects in the long-run.

1. Building a human inventory of awareness, knowledge and skill to manage critical marketing activities like market research and forecasting, product innovation and standardization, pricing methodology, market networking and communication, technological upgradation and advertisement and publicity etc. through adaptation, alteration, and adjustment of indigenous knowledge and skill. Formal education level also needs to be improved through evening classes etc.
2. Providing autonomy and equipping government agencies like DIC and training development institutes with more resources to organize and develop capacity building, technology dissemination, product and design development, and credit and market facilitation.
3. Promotion of SHGs for collective marketing practices.
4. Quality development and standardization of products.
5. Market facilitation through exposure visits and backward and forward stakeholder interaction.
6. Development of specialization of skill and knowledge.
7. Dissemination, expansion and diversification of experience and knowledge of successful and master craftsmen and marketers.

Endnotes

1. Nerys, F., M. Peter, T. Dennis and Andrew H. (2006), "Entrepreneurship and Rural Economic Development: A Scenario Analysis Approach", *International Journal of Entrepreneurial Behaviour and Research,* Vol. 12, No. 5, pp. 289-305.
2. Prahalad, C.K. (2006), "The Fortune at the Bottom of the Pyramid", Wharton School Publishing.
3. Kahn, H. (1962), "Thinking about the Unthinkable", Avon Books, New York, NY.
4. OECD (1996), "Better Policies for Rural Development", Paris,

Organisation for Economic Co-operation and Development.
5. Drabenstott, M., N. Novack and B. Abraham (2003), "Main Streets of Tomorrow: Growing and Financing Rural Entrepreneurs: A Conference Summary", *Economic Review Quarterly,* III: 73-85.
6. Merrett, C.D. and J. J. Gruidl (2000), "Small Business Ownership in Illinois: The Effect of Gender and Location on Entrepreneurial Success", *Professional Geographer*, 52(3): 425-436.
7. Flora, C.B., J. Flora, J. D. Spears, L.E. Swanson, M.B. Lapping and M.L. Weinberg (1992), "Rural Communities: Legacy and Change", Boulder, CO: Westview Press.
8. Kinsley, M.J. (1997), "Economic Renewal Guide: A Collaborative Process for Sustainable Community Development", Snowmass, CO: Rocky Mountain Institute.
9. Miller, N.J. and T.L. Besser (2000), "The Importance of Community Values in Small Business Strategy Formation: Evidence from Rural Iowa", *Journal of Small Business*, pp. 342-360.
10. Nerys, F., M. Peter, T. Dennis and Andrew H. (2006), "Entrepreneurship and Rural Economic Development: A Scenario Analysis Approach", *International Journal of Entrepreneurial Behaviour and Research,* Vol. 12, No. 5, pp. 289-305.
11. Reardon, T., K. Stamoulis, M. Cruz, A. Balisacan, J. Berdegue and B. Banks (1998), "Rural Non-farm Income in Developing Countries", in FAO, 'The State of Food and Agriculture, 1998', Part III, Rome, Food and Agriculture Organization of UN.
12. Christensen, G. and R. Lacroix (1997), "Competitiveness and Employment: A Framework for Rural Development in Poland", World Bank Discussion Paper No. 383, Washington D.C., World Bank.
13. Tahori K. and S. Singh (1993), "Rural Industrialization: A Plan for the Future", second revised edition, Vikas Publishing House, New Delhi.
14. Kashyap, P. and S. Raut (2006), "The Rural Marketing", Biztantra Publications.

13

Growth and Performance of MSMEs

Setaka Palaka and Sandhyarani Das

Introduction

Micro, small and medium enterprises (MSMEs), including khadi and village industries generate the highest rates of employment growth and account for a significant share of industrial production and exports. They also play a key role in the development of the economies with their effective, efficient, flexible, diverse and innovative entrepreneurial spirit. The socio-economic policies adopted by India since the Industries (Development and Regulation) Act, 1951 have laid stress on MSMEs as a means to accelerate the country's economic development.

These enterprises produce a diverse range of products with very simple products, produced by household enterprises at one end of the spectrum and highly advanced ones at the other end. With globalisation and changes in communication technologies, new challenges and opportunities have grown for the MSMEs. The concept and techniques of marketing have also been continuously undergoing a change with rapid changes in technology and consumer preferences.

World over, the MSMEs are recognized as an important constituent of the national economies, contributing significantly to inclusive development and poverty alleviation. Recognising their importance, the Central and State Governments of India have been implementing several schemes and programmes for their promotion and development. The primary responsibility of promotion and development of MSMEs is of the State governments.

However, the Government of India, supplements the efforts

of the States through various initiatives. The measures undertaken by the Ministry of MSMEs and its organisations seek to facilitate adequate flow of credit from financial institutions, support for technology upgradation and modernisation; integrated infrastructural facilities; access to modern management practices; entrepreneurship development and skill upgradation through appropriate training facilities; support for product development, welfare of artisans and workers; assistance for better access to domestic and export markets and cluster-wise measures to promote capacity building and empowerment of the units.

As is elsewhere, in Odisha, the MSMEs are quite diverse and contribute significantly to economic prosperity, employment expansion, regional balance and inclusive development. In this context, it is necessary to analyse the trends in the growth of such enterprises, and their investment and employment in Odisha. The processes of economic reforms and supportive policies for large scale industrialisation of the state, particularly since 1991, have contributed to the development of MSMEs. What has been the nature and trend of the growth of MSMEs since the introduction of economic liberalization in Odisha constitutes to the research problem in this study.

According to the MSMEs Act, 2006, the enterprises are broadly classified in terms of activity such as enterprises engaged in manufacturing, production and enterprises engaged in services. The classification of MSMEs is shown in Figure 13.1.

Literature Review

Singh et al. (2012) analyzed the performance of small-scale industries in India and focused on policy changes which have opened new opportunities for this sector. Their study concluded that SSI sector has made good progress in terms of the number of SSI units, production and employment levels. The study recommended the emergence of technology development and strengthening of financial infrastructure to boost SSI and to achieve the growth target.

Venkatesh and Muthiah (2012) found that the role of small and medium enterprises (SMEs) in the industrial sector is growing rapidly and they have become a thrust area for future growth. They emphasized that nurturing SME sector is essential for the economic well-being of the nation. The above literature highlights the various aspects viz. performance, growth and problems of MSMEs in the Indian economy and induces for continuous research in this field.

Figure 13.1: Classification of MSMEs

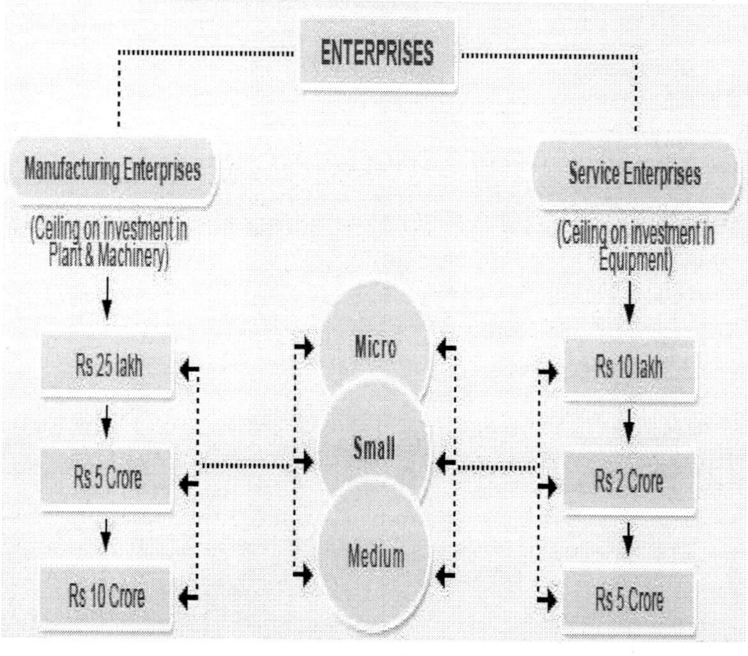

Dixit and Pandey (2011) applied co-integration analysis to examine the causal relationship between SMEs output, exports, employment, number of SMEs and their fixed investment and India's GDP, total exports and employment (public and private) for the period 1973-74 to 2006-07. Their study revealed a positive causality between SMEs output and

India's GDP.

Bhabani T.A. (2010) highlights the issue of quality employment generation by the SSIs and negates the short-term attitude of increasing the volume of employment generation by compromising with quality. The author argues that employment generation by the SSIs may be high in quantitative term but very low in quality. Technological upgradation would enable the small firms to create quality employment, improving remuneration, duration and skills. This structural shift may reduce the rate of employment generation in the short-run but would ensure high-income employment generation in the long-run.

Bargal et al. (2009) examined the causal relationship among the three variables GDP, SSI output and SSI exports and have also compared the performance parameters of SSIs in the pre- and post-liberalization era. The study found that the annual average growth rate of different parameters of SSIs have declined in the period of nineties vis-à-vis the pre-reform years. There is an absence of any lead-lag causal relationship between exports and production in small-scale sector and GDP of the Indian economy.

Sonia and Kansai Rajeev (2009) studied the effects of globalization on micro, small and medium enterprises (MSMEs) during pre- and post-liberalization period from 1973-74 to 2008-09. They used four economic parameters namely number of units, production, employment and exports and interpreted the study results based on annual average growth rate (AAGR) calculation. AAGR in pre-liberalization period (1973-74 to 1989-90) was higher in all selected parameters than that of post-liberalization period (1991-92 to 2007-08). They concluded that MSMEs failed to put up an impressive performance in post-reforms era.

Bala Subrahmanya (2004) highlighted the impact of globalization and domestic reforms on small-scale industries. The study stated that small industry had suffered in terms of growth of units, employment, output and exports. The researcher highlighted that the policy changes had also thrown open new opportunities and markets for the small-scale industries sector. He suggested that focus must be turned to technology development and strengthening of financial infrastructure in order to make Indian small industry internationally competitive and contribute to national income and employment.

Mali (1998) observed that small and medium enterprises (SMEs) and micro enterprises have to face increasing competition in the present scenario of globalization; they have to specifically improve themselves in the fields of management, marketing, product diversification, infrastructural development, and technological up-gradation. Moreover, new small and medium enterprises may have to move from slow growth area to a high growth area and they have to form strategic alliance with entrepreneurs of neighbouring countries. Databank on industries to guide the prospective entrepreneurs including investors from abroad is also essential.

Sandesara (1993) studied the performance of SSIs producing reserved items by collecting data from the Second Census conducted by the Ministry of SSIs. The study examined the null hypothesis that SSI firms producing reserved category items should perform better than SSIs producing non-reserved items. The study result revealed that capacity utilization in 1987-88 and aggregate change in production in 1987-88 were both lower for reserved than for unreserved items. This below par performance of the SSI firms producing reserved items was surprising as those firms did not have to face competition from large firms. The author observed that this could be due to the entrance of excess SSI firms into the protected areas.

Objectives and Methodology of the Study

The study intends to address the issue of growth of MSMEs in Odisha. The specific objectives are the following:

1. To examine the trends in the growth of MSMEs in Odisha in terms of registered units, and their investment and

employment;

2. To analyse the trends of growth of MSMEs in different districts of the state; and
3. To assess the impact of economic reforms on the growth of MSMEs in Odisha.

For this study, data was collected mainly from secondary sources. The information was collected from different books, journals, magazines, articles, published annual reports of the MSME sector, unpublished theses, and newspapers. The district-wise time series data on MSMEs of Odisha was processed for the period from 2001 to 2011.

The collected data were processed using statistical and econometric tools such as percentages, cumulative frequency, trend analysis, growth index etc. The annual compound growth rates have been estimated through the semi-log models as given in Gujarati (2010). The MS Excel computer software was used to estimate the relevant statistical output.

Growth of Registered Units, Investment and Employment in MSMEs in Odisha

A total of 31,212 MSME units were registered in all the 30 districts of Odisha from the year 1985-86 to 2001-2011. The lowest registered units were 708 in the year 1991-92 and the highest figure of 1,708 was registered in 2009-10. The number of registered units was seen to be fluctuating every year.

The cumulative figure had reached 31,212 units in 2010-11 from 1,058 units in 1985-86. The number of registered units had increased since the late 1990s, mainly due to economic reforms and liberalization. The total average employment per unit was 250.76.

The changing patterns of regional dispersion of MSMEs in Odisha during 2010-11 were analysed in this section and it shows the district-wise registered MSME units for 2 selected periods such as 2000-01 and 2001-11.

In 2000-01, the highest number of units were registered in Cuttack district (156 units) and the lowest was in Deogarh district (2 units). In that year, the total registered units in the state were 1,502.

In 2000-01, the highest growth index was 1,700 in Boudh district and the lowest growth was 47 in Sundargarh district. In 2001-11, the highest number of 177 units was registered in Cuttack district and lowest registration of only one unit was witnessed in Malkangiri district. The highest growth index of 6,857 was noticed in Kalahandi, which is a backward district. The district-wise MSME registered units and the cumulative registered units for two selected periods years are presented in Tables 13.1 and 13.2.

Table 13.1: District-wise MSMEs Registered Units for Two Selected Periods

District	2000-01	2001-11
Angul	34 (213)	70 (438)
Balasore	103 (381)	94 (348)
Bargarh	58 (644)	14 (156)
Bolangir	34 (79)	55 (1280)
Boudh	17 (1700)	15 (1500)
Cuttack	156 (173)	177 (197)
Deogarh	2 (100)	15 (750)
Dhenkanal	45 (281)	58 (325)
Gajapati	35 (1167)	11 (367)
Ganjam	119 (108)	100 (91)
Jagatsinghpur	46 (460)	48 (480)
Jajpur	76 (543)	85 (907)
Jharsuguda	23 (576)	22 (550)
Kalahandi	34 (425)	55 (6875)
Kandhamal	31 (775)	42 (1050)
Kendrapara	39 (650)	51 (850)
Keonjhar	63 (700)	78 (867)
Khorda	90 (93)	116 (132)
Koraput	62 (289)	44 (200)
Malkangiri	6 (100)	1 (17)
Mayurbhanj	88 (169)	100 (192)
Nabarangpur	32 (100)	30 (94)
Nayagarh	11 (579)	40 (211)
Nuapada	10 (125)	6 (75)
Puri	55 (611)	71 (789)

Contd...

Rayagada	46 (170)	59 (227)
Sambalpur	45 (225)	20 (100)
Sonepur	22 (1100)	8 (400)
Subarnapur	22 (1100)	8 (400)
Sundargarh	98 (47)	104 (50)

Source: Calculated from information at www.msmedicuttack.gov.in.

Table 13.2: District-wise Cumulative MSME Registered Units for Two Selected Periods

District	2000-01	2001-11
Angul	275 (205)	880 (657)
Balasore	928 (353)	1892 (719)
Bargarh	400 (278)	769 (534)
Bolangir	522 (174)	918 (306)
Boudh	114 (356)	218 (681)
Cuttack	1686 (210)	3323 (414)
Deogarh	43 (215)	133 (665)
Dhenkanal	299 (163)	845 (457)
Gajapati	232 (261)	445 (500)
Ganjam	1199 (263)	2664 (584)
Jagatsinghpur	273 (284)	811 (845)
Jajpur	487 (366)	1807 (1359)
Jharsuguda	235 (233)	528 (523)
Kalahandi	358 (172)	854 (411)
Kandhamal	243 (386)	563 (894)
Kendrapara	236 (513)	665 (1446)
Keonjhar	483 (345)	560 (400)
Khorda	1907 (219)	2815 (324)
Koraput	618 (330)	1133 (606)
Malkangiri	140 (933)	164 (1093)
Mayurbhanj	694 (233)	1707 (573)
Nabarangpur	32 (100)	463 (1447)
Nayagarh	228 (146)	525 (337)
Nuapada	110 (200)	179 (325)
Puri	482 (269)	1111 (621)
Rayagada	426 (398)	901 (842)
Sambalpur	440 (207)	679 (319)
Sonepur	120 (308)	177 (454)
Subarnapur	120 (308)	177 (454)
Sundargarh	2063 (219)	2975 (315)

Source: Calculated from information at www.msmedicuttack.gov.in.

Table 13.3 shows the annual compound growth rate and cumulative frequency of MSME units in Odisha.

Table 13.3:.Annual Compound Growth Rate and Cumulative Frequency of MSMEs in Odisha (percent)

Year	Growth rates	
	Registered Unit	Cumulative frequency of Registered Unit
2001-11	0.55	4.33

Source: Estimated from secondary time series data collected from the website of MSME-Development Institute, Cuttack during 2013.

Employment in MSMEs

Tables 13.4 and 13.5 present the district-wise employment and its cumulative frequency.

Table 13.4: District-wise Employment in MSMEs and Growth indicators for Two Selected Periods

District	2000-01	2001-11
Angul	227 (220)	411 (399)
Balasore	533 (288)	565 (305)
Bargarh	324 (279)	380 (328)
Bolangir	223 (29)	685 (89)
Boudh	134 (2233)	193 (3217)
Cuttack	1369 (133)	2351 (229)
Deogarh	33 (100)	84 (256)
Dhenkanal	210 (333)	448 (711)
Gajapati	328 (1491)	395 (1795)
Ganjam	577 (87)	622 (94)
Jagatsinghpur	326 (604)	250 (463)
Jajpur	434 (270)	533 (343)
Jharsuguda	264 (587)	301 (6689)
Kalahandi	306 (1177)	420 (1615)
Kandhamal	152 (490)	261 (842)
Kendrapara	171 (534)	292 (913)
Keonjhar	455 (299)	783 (515)
Khorda	921 (144)	1940 (303)
Koraput	611 (262)	449 (193)
Malkangiri	25 (100)	2 (8)
Mayurbhanj	673 (123)	1391 (255)
Nabarangpur	210 (100)	240 (114)
Nayagarh	98 (81)	315 (206)
Nuapada	46 (177)	125 (481)
Puri	372 (1094)	810 (2382)

Contd...

Rayagada	241 (41)	894 (153)
Sambalpur	267 (85)	141 (45)
Sonepur	99 (762)	50 (387)
Subarnapur	99 (762)	50 (387)
Sundargarh	606 (27)	1424 (65)

Source: Calculated from information at www.msmedicuttack.gov.in.

Table 13.5: District-wise Cumulative Employment in MSMEs for Two Selected Periods

District	2000-01	2001-11
Angul	1878 (190)	5508 (559)
Balasore	7501 (267)	13887 (495)
Bargarh	3943 (208)	7629 (402)
Bolangir	6111 (174)	9988 (284)
Boudh	835 (10438)	1857 (23213)
Cuttack	18053 (193)	35025 (374)
Deogarh	265 (308)	711 (827)
Dhenkanal	2242 (162)	5629 (407)
Gajapati	2659 (298)	4941 (553)
Ganjam	9693 (254)	19417 (508)
Jagatsinghpur	2328 (228)	5146 (503)
Jajpur	3750 (231)	9563 (588)
Jharsuguda	2270 (206)	4638 (420)
Kalahandi	2989 (175)	7876 (460)
Kandhamal	1090 (281)	2483 (640)
Kendrapara	1292 (285)	3445 (759)
Keonjhar	4385 (288)	9702 (638)
Khorda	21503 (208)	31862 (308)
Koraput	5547 (292)	11257 (592)
Malkangiri	700 (833)	839 (999)
Mayurbhanj	6009 (219)	14298 (522)
Nabarangpur	210 (100)	2854 (1359)
Nayagarh	1590 (141)	3363 (298)
Nuapada	1005 (239)	1718 (409)
Puri	3868 (197)	8576 (436)
Rayagada	3689 (233)	7947 (501)
Sambalpur	4873 (195)	6455 (258)
Sonepur	928 (319)	1728 (594)
Subarnapur	928 (319)	1728 (594)
Sundargarh	20783 (212)	33201 (339)

Source: Calculated from information at www.msmedicuttack.gov.in.

The annual compound growth rate and frequency of employment is presented in Table 13.6.

Table 13.6: Annual Compound Growth Rate and Cumulative Frequency in MSMEs of Odisha (percent)

Year	Growth rates	
	Employment	Cumulative frequency
2001-11	7.67	6.89

Source: Estimated from secondary time series data collected from the website of MSME-Development Institute, Cuttack during 2013.

Investments in MSMEs

District-wise investment in MSMEs and cumulative investment is presented in Tables 13.7 and 13.8 for 2 selected periods. Table 13.8 shows that in 2001-11, total cumulative investment was ₹ 1,60,932.74 lakh with the highest being in Sundargarh district and lowest being in Malkangiri district. The highest growth index was in Nabarangpur district and lowest growth index was in Nuapada district.

Table 13.7: District-wise Investment in MSMEs for Two Selected Years

(₹ lakh)

District	2000-01	2001-11
Angul	114.09 (334.38)	354.52 (1039.04)
Balasore	155.55 (217.10)	672.1 (938.03)
Bargarh	139.31 (45.35)	373.66 (121.63)
Bolangir	102.13 (67.58)	387.65 (256.52)
Boudh	62.00 (103333.33)	322.88 (538133.33)
Cuttack	545.61 (177.42)	2031.75 (660.69)
Deogarh	2.91 (100)	210.22 (7224.05)
Dhenkanal	34.71 (266.39)	174.51 (1339.29)
Gajapati	41.23 (1070.91)	47.2 (1225.97)
Ganjam	141.29 (151.21)	693.2 (741.87)
Jagatsinghpur	55.04 (1030.71)	51.18 (958.43)
Jajpur	82.16 (93.86)	107.52 (122.84)
Jharsuguda	153.41 (9771.34)	498.72 (31765.61)
Kalahandi	193.88 (3425.44)	374.11 (6609.72)
Kandhamal	50.71 (451.96)	147.03 (1310.43)
Kendrapara	28.03 (405.64)	80.86 (1170.19)
Keonjhar	323.99 (973.82)	831.22 (2498.41)
Khorda	535.18 (215.36)	3767.37 (1515.98)
Koraput	68.5 (79.40)	165.92 (192.33)

Contd...

Malkangiri	1.96 (100)	0.08 (4.08)
Mayurbhanj	107.05 (112.39)	1255.4 (1318.00)
Nabarangpur	2.27 (100)	795.46 (35042.29)
Nayagarh	16.5 (112.55)	89.48 (610.37)
Nuapada	8.48 (149.82)	188.6 (3332.16)
Puri	30.27 (104.99)	120.51 (418.00)
Rayagada	61.7 (50.13)	754.00 (612.66)
Sambalpur	95.92 (97.34)	131.06 (133.00)
Sonepur	14.01 (2501.79)	10.42 (1860.71)
Subarnapur	14.01 (2501.79)	10.42 (1860.71)
Sundargarh	300.89 (34.03)	2091.22 (236.51)

Table 13.8: District-wise Cumulative Investment in MSMEs for Two Selected Periods

(₹ lakh)

District	2000-01	2001-11
Angul	514.31 (317.22)	3608.84 (2225.89)
Balasore	3883.21 (234.34)	7373.83 (225.56)
Bargarh	504.25 (100.00)	1834.76 (363.86)
Bolangir	1828.47 (316.83)	8418.25 (1458.69)
Boudh	100.65 (1441.98)	828.14 (11864.47)
Cuttack	5645.55 (301.71)	18787.14 (1004.03)
Deogarh	52.88 (640.97)	671.6 (8140.61)
Dhenkanal	616.68 (285.28)	3551.26 (1642.81)
Gajapati	428.18 (344.20)	889.44 (714.98)
Ganjam	3453.51 (460.64)	7771.42 (1036.57)
Jagatsinghpur	297.86 (257.37)	1896.57 (1638.79)
Jajpur	800.75 (323.91)	3345.36 (1353.25)
Jharsuguda	690.47 (303.74)	3671.55 (1615.15)
Kalahandi	1113.19 (264.96)	4689.26 (1116.15)
Kandhamal	209.51 (486.21)	1029.28 (2388.67)
Kendrapara	278.36 (752.12)	1198.23 (3237.58)
Keonjhar	1430.97 (363.10)	7442.04 (1888.36)
Khorda	8971.47 (341.00)	20469.23 (778.02)
Koraput	1364.45 (243.66)	3325.29 (593.83)
Malkangiri	111.58 (929.06)	148.27 (1234.55)
Mayurbhanj	1451.12 (277.37)	5096.14 (974.09)
Nabarangpur	2.27 (100.00)	7585.62 (334168.28)
Nayagarh	1819.03 (1511.58)	2392.5 (1988.12)
Nuapada	1008.32 (117.95)	1548.84 (181.18)
Puri	460.22 (344.94)	1284.39 (962.67)
Rayagada	976.01 (342.93)	3958.14 (1390.72)
Sambalpur	1562.49 (333.04)	3087.61 (658.11)
Sonepur	128.23 (274.76)	914.85 (1960.25)
Subarnapur	128.23 (274.76)	914.85 (1960.25)
Sundargarh	8532.14 (280.57)	33200.04 (1091.77)
Total	48364.36	160932.74

Annual compound growth rate and cumulative frequency of MSMEs is presented in Table 13.9.

Table 13.9: Annual Compound Growth rate and Cumulative Frequency in MSMEs of Odisha (percent)

Year	Growth rates	
	Investment	Cumulative frequency
2001-11	12.03	13.02

Source: Estimated from secondary time series data collected from the website of MSME-Development Institute, Cuttack during 2013.

The compound growth rates of investment were 12.03 percent and for cumulative figures, 13.02 percent respectively for the above periods.

Conclusions

The analysis has been made in respect of the registered units, and their investment and employment both for the current years and the cumulative figures for the entire state and its 30 districts. It has been found that the districts, which may have large scale industries like Sundargarh, Jharsuguda and Jajpur have a good number of MSMEs. The coastal districts like Ganjam, Khorda and Cuttack also have a large number of small enterprises. This reflects the higher state of economic development in these areas. However, interior districts, like Boudh, Gajapati, Kondhamal, Malkangiri, Nabangpur, Sonepur and Sambalpur are not well-developed with respect to MSMEs. However, all the districts and the state itself has registered a significant positive growth with respect to the chosen indicators of MSMEs, such as registered units, investment and employment.

References

Bala Subrahmanya, M.H. (2004), "Small Industry and Globalization: Implications, Performance and Prospects", *Economic and Political Weekly*, Volume XXXIX, No. 18, pp. 1826-1834.

Bargal, H., M. Dashmishra and A. Sharma (2009), "Performance

Analysis of Small Scale Industry: A Study of Pre-liberalization and Post-liberalization Period", *International Journal of Business and Management*, Vol. 1, No. 2.

Bhabani, T.A. (2010), "Dynamic Business Environments: What These Mean for Indian Small Enterprises", in Keshab Das (ed.), 'Micro and Small Enterprises in India: An Era of Reforms'.

Bhandare, S.S. (2001), "WTO and Indian Industry", *Forum of Free Enterprises*, No. 2, Mumbai, February-March, p. 2.

Bhat, T.P. et al. (2000), "Impact of WTO Agreement on Small and Medium Enterprises in India", *The Indian Journal of Commerce*, Vol. 53, No. 122, New Delhi, January-June.

Biswasroy, P.K. and P. Devi Mishra (1992), "The Dynamics of Small-scale Industries: An Overview", SEDME, Vol. XXX, No. 2, June, pp. 36-37.

Cheruniluam, F. (1984), "Industrial Economics: Indian Perspective", Sauharda Publisher, Mysore, p. 1.

Dixit, A. and A.K. Pandey (2011), "SMEs and Economic Growth in India: Cointegration Analysis", *The IUP Journal of Financial Economics*, Vol. IX, No. 2, pp. 41-59.

Dutta, R.C. (1960), "Economic History of India in Victorian Age: 1837-1900", Publication Division, Delhi.

Gujarati, D.N. (2003), "Basic Econometrics", fourth edition, Tata McGraw-Hill, New Delhi, pp. 178-181.

Kavinde, D.J. (1980), "Five Year Plan and SSI", *SBI Monthly Review*, January.

Kranti, L. (1992), "Economic Development and Planning", Lakshmi Narain Aggarwal Educational Publishers, Agra, p. 28.

Krishna, K.L. (1987), "Industrial Growth and Productivity in India", in P.R. Brahmananda and V.R. Panchamukhi (eds.), 'The Development of the Indian Economy', Himalaya Publishing House, Delhi, p. 348.

Kuchhal, S.C. (1978), "Major Indian Industries", Chaitanya Publishing House, Allahabad.

Mali, D.D. (1998), "Development of Micro, Small and Medium Enterprises of India: Current Scenario and Challenges", *SEDME (Small Enterprises Development, Management and Extension) Journal*, Vol. 25, No. 4.

Mukhi, H.R. (1983), "Industrial Economy with Special Reference to India", New Heights Publishers, New Delhi.

Naroji, D. (1901), "Poverty and Un-British Rule in India", Swansonn

Enchien, London.

Patra, G.S., P.C. Mishra and G.S. Lall (2006), "Financing Small Scale Industry", Discovery Publishing House, New Delhi.

Patra G.L. and P.C. Mishra P.C., (2003) *Institutional Financing for Small Scale Industries*, Discovery Publishing House, New Delhi.

Planning Commission, Ninth Five Year Plan (1997-2002), Vol. II, p.576.

Raju, B Yerram; Fortifying Small Sector the Challenges, Indian Management, Vol. 9 No. 8, august 2000, Bombay, pp. 43-49.

Singh, R., Verma, O.P., and Anjum, B. (2012), 'Small Scale Industry: An Engine of Growth, Zenith International Journal of Business Economics & Management Research, Vol. 2 Issue 5, Online available at http://www.zenithresearch.org.in.

Venkatesh, S. and Muthiah, K, (2012), 'SMEs in India: Importance and Contribution', Asian Journal 9of Management Research, Vol. 2, No. 2.

Index